CROSSING THE DIGITAL FAULTLINE

SRI MANCHALA

CROSSING THE DIGITAL FAULTLINE

10 RULES
OF HIGHLY SUCCESSFUL LEADERS IN DIGITALIZATION

SECOND EDITION

ForbesBooks

Published by ForbesBooks, Charleston, South Carolina.
Member of Advantage Media Group.

ForbesBooks is a registered trademark, and the ForbesBooks colophon is a trademark of Forbes Media, LLC.

Printed in the United States of America.

10 9 8 7 6 5 4 3 2 1

ISBN: 978-1-950863-74-7
LCCN: 2021909937

This custom publication is intended to provide accurate information and the opinions of the author in regard to the subject matter covered. It is sold with the understanding that the publisher, Advantage|ForbesBooks, is not engaged in rendering legal, financial, or professional services of any kind. If legal advice or other expert assistance is required, the reader is advised to seek the services of a competent professional.

Advantage Media Group is proud to be a part of the Tree Neutral® program. Tree Neutral offsets the number of trees consumed in the production and printing of this book by taking proactive steps such as planting trees in direct proportion to the number of trees used to print books. To learn more about Tree Neutral, please visit **www.treeneutral.com**.

Since 1917, Forbes has remained steadfast in its mission to serve as the defining voice of entrepreneurial capitalism. ForbesBooks, launched in 2016 through a partnership with Advantage Media Group, furthers that aim by helping business and thought leaders bring their stories, passion, and knowledge to the forefront in custom books. Opinions expressed by ForbesBooks authors are their own. To be considered for publication, please visit **www.forbesbooks.com**.

Dedicated to every board member, CEO, and business and IT leader on the front lines of transformation battles as they persevere and reinvent their companies and organizations to be relevant and thrive in the long run.

I wish you all the very best in this challenge of a lifetime—made even harder with the COVID-19 pandemic. With the right mindset and a methodical, data-driven approach, I have no doubt you will succeed.

■　■　■

With deep appreciation for the research team at Trianz, the Marshall School of Business at the University of Southern California, and our editors for their contributions; all associates and leaders at Trianz for their execution of our own transformation strategies and demonstrating unflinching commitment to our clients even during COVID-19; and to my wife, Laxmi, and our entire family for their support, encouragement, and a cheerful family environment during a very challenging time for all leaders.

CONTENTS

PART II: THE 10 RULES OF HIGHLY SUCCESSFUL LEADERS IN THE DIGITAL AGE

PART III: THE PERSONA OF SUCCESSFUL LEADERS IN THE DIGITAL AGE

PART IV: APPLYING THE 10 RULES: THE METHODICAL INNOVATOR'S PLAYBOOK

FIGURES

TABLES

INTRODUCTION

Humans have a limited capacity for change. When this capacity is overwhelmed, the consequence is future shock.
—ALVIN TOFFLER, *FUTURE SHOCK* (1970)

For more than two decades, changes powered by digitalization have been sweeping across all governments, industries, and human, plant, and animal ecosystems throughout the world. These changes manifest in various forms—in a host of new social behaviors, revolutionary products and services, and entirely new technology companies that are reframing established business paradigms. Commercials from electric toothbrushes to gaming, furniture to reconfigurable homes, embedded health devices to electric cars—all bring "digital transformation" to full life in a few seconds.

Indeed, no business is immune to these dramatic, foundational, and deeply intertwined shifts. But even after spending enormous amounts of effort and capital on digitalization, our research shows that more than 90 percent of organizations fail or show poor results in adjusting to the rapidly changing business environment. Our analysis further predicts that more than 30 percent of companies will cease to exist by the end of this decade—a trend that will only speed up in the coming years.

Today, every board member, CEO, and business and IT leader is on the fault line of this earthquake of change. They work feverishly to survive the onslaught of digitalization by reinventing their organizations as fast as they can. But when the computer is shut down and the lights are switched off at the day's end, however, every leader has the same questions: Are we on the right track? Are we doing things that are going to make a difference? Are we moving at the right pace? Will we make it?

We are now in that state of future shock.

The seeds of this book were planted years ago as our own company pivoted to digital transformations. It was brought to harvest through data-driven research, experience, and interviews with many leaders. I began to study digitalization in late 2016 to help our company make its own transition and to be able to advise clients on their digitalization. Spread over three-plus years under the umbrella of the Trianz Global Transformation Study (TGTS), we collected data from more than five thousand large, medium, and small companies. These surveys covered every major business and IT function from twenty industries worldwide.

In *Crossing the Digital Faultline*, I share a data-driven understanding of the upheavals of the digital-transformation game, what I call the "Digital Faultline." I show why only 7 percent of leaders succeed in adapting to the change in business caused by this transformation and provide management tools to help you confidently chart your course for the future as one of those who will succeed. To be clear, this book is not about technology and how it is a panacea to the challenge of change. Rather, it looks at transformations from the perspective of customers and businesses, and it positions technology as a means to an end and not an end in itself. It is about the human dimension and leadership techniques that are essential for taming this challenge of a lifetime and succeeding in the Digital Age.

State of Digital Transformations: It Is Early, but the Game Is Evolving Rapidly

Contrary to the endless hype, the digital-transformation game has only just begun, but it is gaining momentum around the world. Even though COVID-19 has accelerated the pace, the Trianz Global Transformation Survey (TGTS) data shows that it is not too late to get in the game:

Fewer than 10 percent of B2B or B2C products and services have transformed to provide new value propositions and a digitalized experience. These experiences are web, app, or Internet-of-Things-driven (IoT-driven), with high levels of automation and low or no human interaction.

Fewer than 25 percent of business processes across companies have been properly aligned or digitalized. They are not yet connected or optimized to provide great experiences to stakeholders, such as customers, employees, partners, suppliers, and regulators.

More than 70 percent of companies fail to fully understand or use the analytics required for digital transformations. Analytics will be the number one area of investment in the years to come.

While marketing will continue receiving attention, R&D and human capital will see the highest level of investments.

Only 4–7 percent of companies succeed in digitaliza-

> Analytics will be the number one area of investment in the years to come.

tion and are producing superior business performance. While the pace is picking up due to COVID-19, the other 93 percent must quickly transform to stay in the fight for customer relevance and market share.

Separately, TGTS data shows a phenomenon called "industry tech," or the "born digitals." This involves whole groups of start-up companies developing disruptive new value propositions. Their entire value for the customer, engagement, and interactions are fully digitalized. An industry-tech start-up can either be a new company (such as Tesla, Ring, Airbnb, or Lyft) or a well-funded consortium of existing companies.

TGTS data shows that large and medium organizations with established business models transform slowly due to several factors. Among these factors are a lack of comprehension by top management, nonalignment, and cultures of incumbency based on long-standing relationships with other players in their industry. In many established companies, there is a clear lack of technological savvy and a general contest between the old and the new way of doing things. No matter what the reason or size or brand, this general inertia leads to irreversible decline and demise in the digital era.

On the other hand, Silicon Valley, California, and now Redmond, Washington, and tech in general—which are not just the catalysts of digital transformations but the authors of its next challenge—continue to thrive. Why is that the case? How is it that the business world has become divided into the technology haves and have-nots? Why is tech able to select where and when it wants to take over an industry and do it successfully—again and again and again?

While there are many growing examples of companies that have successfully transformed in other industries as well, tech, as a rule, does exceptionally well. It is no longer affected by downturns or even a pandemic. It has delivered an approximately 20 percent annual return over the past decade, including a mind-boggling 43 percent return in 2020.

Over the past three decades, Silicon Valley or the tech industry in general has garnered a multidimensional "unfair advantage." First, technology is central to digital transformations and the tech industry is in control, writing the script for these transformations. Second, tech companies have access to the adoption and usage data of all their technology by businesses and consumers. They then use this information to steer the course of their companies to "what's next." Finally, they pick and choose market opportunities in other industries that can be digitalized and pursue them at will.

Crossing the Digital Faultline decodes each of these aspects to help nontech companies defend their turf and get even. The good news for leaders in these companies is that this industrial revolution is still in its early stages. However, they must quickly calibrate their company's position on industry-specific transformation trajectories and develop strategies to transform and first survive, then succeed.

The Purpose—A Focus on Leadership in Digitalization and amid High Uncertainty

Our analyses of more than 1.8 million (and growing) data points reveal several macro-level trends on the status and evolution of industries. They show why tech-centric industries, such as hi-tech, telecommunications, media and entertainment, and financial services, are more successful at navigating the digital challenge than are traditional industries. We learned about companies across industries that are prioritizing their investments and approaching the entire life cycle from strategy through implementation and operations.

Along the way, I felt that we should focus on success, not failure, and ask ourselves, "What powers these Digital Champions that are the 7 percent of organizations that are highly successful in their transformation efforts?" We reviewed TGTS data to see what these companies do to develop their vision and priorities, what technologies they adopt and at what pace, various execution models, organizational change, and ways to measure success. We asked whether Digital Champions follow a secret framework and if some leadership models, processes, and styles are more successful than others. At the end of a year-long process that included speaking to several successful clients, one thing became crystal clear: the most critical determinants of successful transformation of a company, unit, business, or IT function are the digital IQ, persona, and the methods its leaders follow.

No other single factor—years of being in business, brand names, market power, intellectual property, technological savvy, revenues, or balance sheets—plays a more important role than the style and approach adopted by a company's leaders.

Successful leaders confront, comprehend, think, act, and perform differently in the Digital Age—and yes, there is a process to it.

What then emerges is a distinct pattern and style of leadership that does not fit into any traditional mold. Digital Champion Leaders are not your charismatic, personality-driven leaders. On the contrary, they are quiet, disciplined, and systematic and take a step-by-step approach while relying heavily on data. The digital IQ and methodical approach that these leaders adopt is acquired over time—showing clearly that such an IQ is not a gift from the heavens or one's mother but an asset and a faculty that is acquired with a lot of hard work. Therefore, I've created a new leadership persona called the "Methodical Innovator" to highlight this style and technique at length so that readers can begin to adapt to a leadership model that is succeeding.

The Flow of Crossing the Digital Faultline

A most profound impact of digitalization is its effect on the human dimension of companies and their shareholder value. As our data predicts, some 30–40 percent of companies across industries will not survive the onslaught of digitalization. Winners will thrive and peel away while losing companies will stagnate and fail. This, in turn, will displace large segments of the workforce and cause a destruction of shareholder value in losing companies. A key motivation of this book is to share data-driven insights on digitalization and present the rules of the game for those who are behind the curve. I hope the insights in this book will help these companies to adapt and drive change before it is too little and too late.

Crossing the Digital Faultline is conversational and organized into four major parts. It begins with an understanding of the current lay of the land, the underlying forces and the journey across, and ends at a point where leaders can regain control and direction.

Part I discusses what the Digital Faultline is and provides an understanding of the invisible and disruptive forces acting beneath the surface. It also shows how businesses will evolve and the available window of opportunity for companies to transform. Forces on the Digital Faultline act much like the laws of physics or mathematics and impact everything in their way without preference or discrimination.

In Part II, we will review the 10 Rules or habits that set apart the 7 percent successful companies (Digital Champions) and their leaders. These 10 Rules are responses by successful leaders in overcoming and then taking advantage of the upheavals. They also determine winners and losers—the creators or recipients of future shock—in the Digital Age.

Part III of the book describes the persona of leaders in Digital Champion organizations. These leaders achieve success by following prescribed steps and then repeating those steps on a continuous basis. This process is crucially augmented by the adoption of what I call the "Methodical Innovator's persona." These leaders are not powered by any particular charisma, magnetism, or political skill. They are also not born with the versatile skills that are critical to succeed in these challenging times. Rather, they are everyday women and men of character who confront the situation squarely and are determined to succeed. They are constant learners who experiment and adapt, orchestrating execution and results relentlessly. In an iterative learning process, they master the 10 Rules. The essence of this book is that everyone has a chance to succeed if they understand this persona and its rules of success.

In Part IV, I present a playbook to help readers to adopt, customize, and practice the persona of a Methodical Innovator. We come to understand their leadership habits and see how they develop a digital vision and execute iteratively. Digital Champions are quick to realize that their success depends entirely on the ability of their teams to execute. The playbook is meant to help in a personal transformation as well as that of your teams.

Crossing the Digital Faultline does not advocate for cool technologies or hypertechnical and futuristic models. Rather, it presents data-driven insights and experiences of successful leaders in a nontechnical way. The goal is to help leaders create a personalized framework for changing themselves and their teams to win the battles ahead.

COVID-19 and Its Effect on Digitalization

I began writing *Crossing the Digital Faultline* in August 2019, and by March 2020, just as COVID-19 hit, the book was ready for publication. But I felt the need to go back to the drawing board to factor in the impact of the pandemic and was quite stunned by what I call the "COVID effect."

In a nutshell, even before COVID-19 hit worldwide, companies were struggling to understand the why, what, when, and how of digital transformations. COVID-19 has disrupted how we work, produce, sell, buy, and deliver to our consumer—at lightning speed. It has cratered a stable revenue and profit environment and rapidly diminished skilled resource pools. This has forced leaders to fight a battle on numerous fronts. Companies must address revenue volatility due to COVID and serious changes in customer behavior. They must usher in a digital way of working and execute with far fewer resources and in a much shorter time window than ever before. The future of survival and rejuvenation is the battle facing leaders—today and now.

Despite this dark time for global businesses and economies, success is still available to leaders. Those who play it aggressively but thoughtfully and know what the battle is all about will ultimately win. The only way to beat the "future shock" from digitalization is to methodically confront, predict, outsmart, and shape the change it causes.

Finally, a few words of advice on how to get the best out of *Crossing the Digital Faultline*. In essence, the book is covering four themes—forces driving digitalization; the ten rules of highly successful leaders; the persona of such leaders or methodical innovators; and finally, a playbook for

> The only way to beat the "future shock" from digitalization is to methodically confront, predict, outsmart, and shape the change it causes.

adopting this persona to drive change. While the language is non-technical and easy to understand, each of these topics is complex and needs time for digestion in order to become a building block for the next. Therefore, I'd suggest a well-paced read with time for making notes and going through the summaries of takeaways placed at the end of key chapters. Once you finish reading a Part, I'd suggest a pause for reflection before moving on to the next Part. This approach I hope will help you absorb learnings of successful leaders and make them actionable for yourself.

So let us get right to it. Our journey begins in Chapter 1: On the Faultline, which shows what it feels like to be in the middle of a real earthquake. We will understand the digital earthquake and the invisible forces causing upheavals on its faultline.

Sri Manchala
Silicon Valley, California
April 2021

PART I
THE DIGITAL FAULTLINE

CHAPTER 1

ON THE FAULTLINE—
FORTY-EIGHT HOURS IN TOKYO

As readers know, the word "faultline" stands for the place where the ground shifts during an earthquake. It can also be called the "ground zero" of an earthquake. The inspiration for this book's title came from my real-life earthquake experience in Tokyo in March 2011.

Tokyo is a convenient stopover when traveling from San Francisco to Singapore or India. It was my fifteenth visit to Japan over the course of a decade, but this one was special for a few reasons. I was with my colleague Ven, who had flown in from Boston to demonstrate our new clinical trials software. The client was the Japanese subsidiary of one of the largest clinical research companies in the world. We had already presented to their teams in India, Singapore, the United States, and Europe. Our meetings in Tokyo and Shanghai were the final stretch, and we were excited at the prospect of finishing our tour on a high note. Ven's brother Swamy had just passed the medical entrance exam, and Ven surprised him with a trip to Japan.

We were staying at the Marriott Hotel in the Ginza district, where our small satellite office in Japan was located. We were met at our hotel by Nomura san, our Japanese colleague. He had been coordinating all discussions with our clients. After we discussed the demo, what questions to expect, how use an interpreter, and logistics for the event, we concluded for the evening. That would be our last peaceful evening in Tokyo.

We met again the next morning at our office at 11:00 a.m. on March 11, 2011, and began final preparations for our client meetings.

Around 1:30 p.m., I felt my desk and computer shaking and looked around. Everyone else felt it too. It was an earthquake, and we hoped it would fade away, but it did not. Acting out of caution, we filed out of the office, went down six floors of stairs, and joined thousands of people out on the street. After five minutes or so, things seemed to return to normal, and we felt it was okay to go back in.

A little after 2:45 p.m., we felt another tremor, only bigger and more violent. The file cabinets were moving, lamps were swinging, the fridge in the kitchen was shaking, and it was clear that this was not something small. I did a quick internet search and saw the breaking news—a massive earthquake had hit Japan minutes earlier. We lost the internet right after I saw the headlines. Instinctively, I asked our office administrator to shut everything down and told everyone to pack their bags and leave the office. We all hurried back into the street.

Tokyo's streets were filled with thousands of workers and residents with confused and nervous looks on their faces. I looked at the skyline and saw the skyscrapers swaying a bit. The ground below us felt like the rubber on a trampoline, flexing and moving. As I looked down the street, everything appeared tilted. The lack of stable ground in those few seconds disturbed the equilibrium in my body, leading to the release of excessive amounts of adrenaline as it prepared for a physical shock. When that expected shock did not happen, the surplus adrenaline filled me with a strange feeling of nausea.

We sent everyone home for their own safety, but I decided that Nomura, Ven, and I should visit the clients' office, as they would be waiting for us. I felt it would be unprofessional to not go and joked with my colleagues that I did not want our Japanese clients to say we chickened out due to a little earthquake.

There were no taxis, buses, or private cars plying the roads, so we walked the three miles to their office. By then, everyone in Tokyo was on the streets but all walking calmly and without hysteria. Mobile phone networks were down. The only sounds we heard were the loud-speakers at street crossings blaring news and instructions in Japanese.

What no one knew at that time was that an 8.8 magnitude earthquake had erupted in Sendai, a coastal town 190 miles north of Tokyo. This was later upgraded to 9.1 by the US Geological Survey.

We were on the faultline—where the next eighteen hours would unfold like a once-in-a-lifetime nightmare. To help you better visualize what that experience was, let me describe the scene as it unfolded hour by hour:

3:00 p.m. Japan Standard Time (JST): My colleagues and I began walking from our offices in Ginza to our client's office three miles away. Due to the magnitude of the quake, we really did not know whether the meeting would take place. When we reached their offices, we found our clients waiting for us, as you would expect of the Japanese.

3:30 p.m.–5:00 p.m. (JST): We met in a large room to demonstrate our technology even as the tables, projector, and computers shook the entire time. Despite this, eight clients listened to the presentation with rapt attention. We ended our meeting with a series of action items. On the way out, we paused in the cafeteria where CNN was breaking news of the massive earthquake, showing the first visuals from ground zero in Sendai.

5:00 p.m.–5:30 p.m. (JST): As we walked back to the Marriott, all of Tokyo was in the streets too, walking in an orderly manner, heads bowed and plodding on. As we plodded toward the hotel, I stared at the display windows of convenience stores; all food on the shelves was gone.

5:30 p.m.–7:00 p.m. (JST): We reached the Marriott, where the business hotel lobby resembled a refugee camp, with desolate-looking elderly Japanese people sitting all over the place with nowhere to go. A quarter of Tokyo's population commutes from the suburbs more than sixty miles away, and because there were no trains, they could not go home. And because they were not prepared to remain overnight, they did not have their daily medications or any food with them. With no cell service, no available food, no medications, and no way to get anywhere except on foot, they were desperate.

We had two rooms at the hotel and, seeing the condition of the elderly, I asked Nomura san to speak to the lobby manager and give up one of our rooms so that the hotel could in turn give it away.

We had anxious moments in our own team. Ven's brother Swamy had gone to explore Tokyo and was nowhere to be found. To everyone's relief, he found his way back to the hotel.

7:00 p.m.–9:00 p.m. (JST): We returned to our one remaining room and enjoyed a makeshift dinner of mixed nuts and snacks from the minibar. Our room was exceptionally small, given that real estate is very expensive in Tokyo. The beds were made for Japanese guests and were much smaller than in typical American hotel rooms. There we were, four of us in one microscopic room in the middle of an unprecedented natural disaster. Dinner was a packet or two of mixed nuts and other dry snacks kept in the room.

9:00 p.m.–10:00 p.m. (JST): Even as I tried to make sense of the whole thing, the safety and security of my team was paramount in my mind. I decided to bring some order and control to our own situation and set up two-hour guard duty shifts for each of us. The idea was that if anything happened, we would wake one another in time to evacuate. I did not sleep at all because one question kept running in my mind—how do I get my team out of Tokyo as soon as possible? The others were not able to sleep properly either due to the two hundred plus aftershocks keeping us on high alert throughout the night.

10:00 p.m.–3:00 a.m. (JST), March 12: Around midnight, CNN began reporting news of an unfolding disaster at the Daiichi Nuclear Power Plant in Fukushima, a town south of Sendai and some 150 miles from Tokyo. A loss of power resulted in overheated fuel rods, which led to several explosions. A nuclear meltdown. That was truly the last thing we needed. Monitoring the Fukushima nuclear plant and "what if" analyses were the continuous theme that night. How long will it be before the reactors would be out of control? How far is Tokyo? Which direction is the wind blowing in? And on and on.

All night, I kept thinking about how to get my team out of Tokyo. I knew I was not responsible for what was happening around us in an earthquake zone with a nuclear reactor melting down. But I was responsible for them being in Tokyo that night and for their safety and well-being.

5:00 a.m.–6:00 a.m. (JST): Internet and cell services were restored. The news of the earthquake and the nuclear disaster was being broadcast everywhere in the world. My inbox filled up with concerned emails, with my wife asking me how we were and our clients asking about our well-being and safety. I let everyone know that we were okay, but I still had no idea how we were going to get to safety. That was all I could think about. The transportation services were still not running. At 4:30 a.m. Nomura san decided to walk home, more than fifty miles.

6:00 a.m.–7:00 a.m. (JST): I went down to the street to see what was happening and what the general chatter was. The nonstop hustle and bustle of Tokyo had been replaced with a deserted, postapocalyptic look and feel. All the shops were shuttered, and there was no one on the streets in any direction. In the lobby, I overheard a rumor that the authorities were considering running a train to Osaka, about 250 miles to the southwest. That was all I needed—a sliver of an opening, the smallest opportunity to pursue to get everyone to safety. At that moment, the farther south we were from Tokyo, the safer we were.

I rushed to our room to tell the guys my plan—we quickly collected our bags and raced out of the hotel. As luck would have it, we spotted a lone brave and enterprising taxi driver cruising through the streets. He graciously took us to the station. The rumor was true— the first bullet train from Tokyo to Osaka was preparing to leave. We bought tickets, ran to the platform, and boarded the train. Minutes later, we were racing away from Tokyo at 270 miles an hour.

Upon reaching Osaka, we called United Airlines, which by then knew what was happening in Japan. They accommodated Swamy on a plane to Boston. Ven and I managed to get on a plane to Shanghai. Nomura reported that his family was safe with relatives. My team was safe, and I could finally think about how to move forward and make sure that our meetings in Shanghai were successful.

Shaken and Stirred: Inversion of Fundamentals on the Faultline

While our experiences in this massive earthquake were nerve-racking, the fundamentals had changed at a big-picture level. In the twenty-four hours from when the earthquake hit until we reached Osaka, life was entirely disrupted. But as an individual or the leader of small team, I had no way of knowing the enormity of the disaster.

Though everyone was indeed calm and orderly, a sense of fear was palpable all around. Order is maintained when all systems are in place and functioning properly. With internet, phone services, taxi, and bus systems all out of service, and train services halted, the only thing that continued to work was the electrical grid.

From the time the second tremor hit at 2:45 p.m. on March 11, we all felt a sense of confusion, nervous helplessness, and a sudden absolute loss of control. We did not even understand the magnitude of what was occurring. Everything on the faultline was dynamic to the extreme. Just when we thought it was a massive earthquake that was over, aftershocks began. A few hours later, Sendai was hit with a tsunami and floods that rose to the height of buildings. Then, when we thought this was restricted to that area, the situation changed yet again with a nuclear meltdown occurring in Fukushima, which was distressingly close to us.

Weeks later, the complete story emerged on how the fundamentals had changed forever. The 2011 Tohoku quake was the fourth strongest in recorded human history. It is incomprehensible that this disaster began when the North American and the Pacific tectonic plates moved a mere two inches. For the uninitiated, these plates run a hundred miles deep and do not normally move at all. The energy released by the friction from these few inches of movement was equal to six hundred million times that of the Hiroshima atomic bomb.

The short- and long-term consequences were enormous. Thousands of people—sometimes entire families—perished. Some $240 billion worth of residential and commercial property and infrastructure were damaged. Northeastern Japan physically moved seven feet east. The Earth's axis shifted by four to ten inches, and to maintain its orbit, the speed of the Earth's rotation increased, reducing the day by 1.8 microseconds.

> Just when we thought it was a massive earthquake that was over, aftershocks began. A few hours later, Sendai was hit with a tsunami and floods that rose to the height of buildings. Then, when we thought this was restricted to that area, the situation changed yet again with a nuclear meltdown occurring in Fukushima, which was distressingly close to us.

In the face of such far-reaching seismic shifts, the leadership question is, how do you make sense of an event of this scope, magnitude, and velocity? How do you react even as it unfolds in front of you, though you can neither see nor control the forces behind it?

The Role of a Leader in a Megacrisis: Lessons from the Faultline

No one can foresee catastrophic events such as the earthquake in Japan, let alone predict their timing, location, direction, or scope. As such events unfold, they are driven by invisible forces, forces we will not have any relevant experience with and which we have no control over—at least initially.

The realization that came from my trip to Tokyo was not a sudden epiphany. It was a reminder that the first thing leaders must do in a crisis is to get their teams to safe harbor. Those who train and serve in the military or other uniformed services know that it is never about you but about the mission and everybody around you.

Metaphorically speaking, we are all on what I call the Digital Faultline today. We all face the same crisis of disruption of the norm, of accelerating digitalization, COVID, and ever-changing technologies. At any moment in this faultline zone, the ground underneath may shift. New business models, products, services, and competitors will destabilize what we have taken for granted.

> The first thing leaders must do in a crisis is to get their teams to safe harbor.

Suddenly, we will have to fight for survival. Information is never complete, accurate, and is sometimes even contradictory and unreliable. While everyone is anxious and nervous on these shifting grounds, successful leaders excel in their swift and thoughtful response to the challenge.

Experienced leaders instinctively show composure, thoughtfulness, quick analysis, and action. In a crisis, composure is as contagious as panic. When leaders are calm and composed in their assessments, decisions, and communications, their team's actions also rise to the challenge.

In Tokyo in 2011, leaders clearly knew that if the crisis grew, there would be more harm to human lives, infrastructure, and the economy. But it is not the economy and infrastructure that they were thinking about. Their first reaction was to contain the damage, ensure public safety, and minimize fatalities. In a small way, mine was to get my team to safety and not about the deal or even the overall business.

The dual threats of digitalization and the COVID pandemic have created a complex and rapidly evolving faultline-like situation.

The next-generation products, services, or business models may not resemble those of the past. Many may not even come from within the industry. Competitors are left guessing about the contours or timing of a new product or service. Such discontinuous shifts will cause enormous upheaval and damage to well-established structures. Companies that are part of that legacy will see dire consequences of widespread challenges if they do not act or react quickly and correctly.

Leaders who have successfully transformed thus far—i.e., the 7 percent—did things differently. They understood that the biggest cost of inaction or failure is an irrecoverable loss of the window of opportunity. At the same time, they understood that no one can get this complex situation right the first time. Success is gained in steps.

> Leaders who have successfully transformed thus far—i.e., the 7 percent—did things differently. They understood that the biggest cost of inaction or failure is an irrecoverable loss of the window of opportunity. At the same time, they understood that no one can get this complex situation right the first time. Success is gained in steps.

As a first step, they calmly deconstruct uncertainties by analyzing the forces causing these upheavals. They outline a vision to address these forces that is easily understood, execute the vision iteratively, and reestablish control. Before painting grand visions, they generate momentum, gain clarity, and succeed steadily and continuously. Each success brings control back and creates valuable learning. Eventually they get a full grip and then view upheavals as opportunities to reposition, follow new rules, disrupt, and win market leadership. These are our Digital Champions.

In effect, highly successful leaders first understand and then steer their organizations away from the Digital Faultline to a point of safety and control.

Let us first take a look at the Digital Faultline and understand the invisible forces acting to create this unprecedented disruption as the successful leaders have done.

CHAPTER 2

FORCES BENEATH THE DIGITAL FAULTLINE

Change is rampant and continuous on the Digital Faultline, sometimes occurring in small increments and at other times on a large scale. The nonstop, bustling activity can be confusing, chaotic, and even frightening. Things no longer conform to the known, structured, and predictable. Fundamentals are inverted, and basic assumptions no longer hold true.

The causes and patterns are unclear in the beginning of the shock. One does not know where they are coming from or where they are leading. This is because while the destruction is visible on the surface, the forces are below the ground and invisible.

Leaders responsible for products, marketing, sales, and services struggle to understand the change while still having to defend their current turf. Leaders in business operations and support functions are in the same boat. They feel the "bullwhip" or cascading effects of revenue and profit volatility. But they have no choice but to rise to the challenge of the Digital Faultline by delegating what they can.

They must deprioritize unimportant tasks and initiatives. They must put in the hours, nights, and weekends—whatever it takes—to step back, learn about, and make sense of the causes of these upheavals.

This chapter uses data from TGTS to explore important drivers beneath the earthquakes across industries (Figure 1). We will see why and how fundamentals change on the faultline, why it is no longer "business as usual," and why old assumptions do not work. Let us review the six major forces described in Figure 1 and make sense of the dynamics, the pace, and the direction of change.

FIGURE 1. TECTONIC FORCES BENEATH THE DIGITAL FAULTLINE

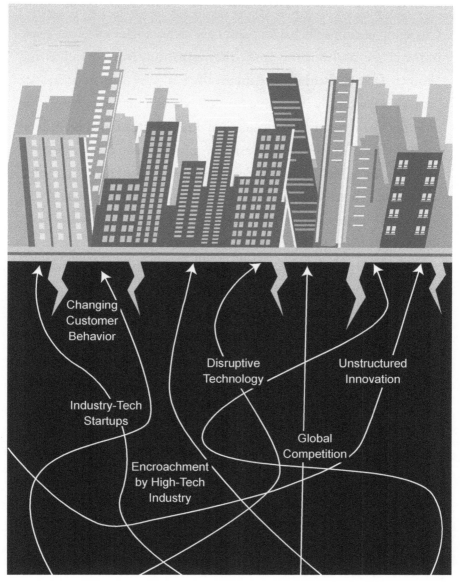

© Trianz Research (Trasers) 2021

Forces 1 and 2—Customer Behavior and Disruptive Technologies: The "Known" Factors

Changing customer behaviors and new technologies affecting every industry are well documented. They constitute what I call as the "known factors" behind the upheavals. I suggest that every reader start diving seriously into these two subjects as a matter of habit. For example, there is a lot of basic material on emerging digital behaviors, preferences, and buying patterns in various customer segments. Similarly, information on the technologies for delivering better value and building better experiences and apps is also easily available. While underlying factors vary by industry, there is enough basic material on these topics to be read and shared with your teams.

However, things are changing very rapidly beyond what is obvious. For example, one lasting impact of the COVID-19 crisis is getting accustomed to isolation. People are safe from infection but also more comfortable and even productive while confined to their homes. A direct consequence of this trend is that people spend more time with electronic devices and computers, whether shopping, connecting with people, seeking entertainment, gaming, or pursuing hobbies in between working sessions.

The *more* time people spend on their devices, the *less* they interact with businesses in person. Companies are struggling to understand their customers' changing behavior because of this new dynamic. Their lack of understanding can have serious ramifications on the very relevance of their products and services.

Similarly, technology is helping to make obsolete existing value propositions while consolidating or creating new ones.

For example, tire manufacturers are experimenting with the concept of smart tires and a "miles-not-tires" business model. Smart tires will carry embedded IoT devices that feed wear and tear data to manufacturers. This creates an opportunity for manufacturers to proactively prompt customers to replace tires that are wearing out. Customers will no longer need to buy tires if they buy guaranteed miles and replacement services. Changing out tires would be an automatic, guaranteed service. The impact of this innovation is that it creates a new direct connection between the tire manufacturers and the end user. It also eliminates the need for tire dealerships and reduces inventories throughout the supply chain. All this sharply increases profits for the tire company while improving customer satisfaction.

A single technology-enabled value proposition can therefore disrupt an entire industry today. If you are the tire manufacturer creating smart tires, then you are setting the agenda for change and are in control. If you are a competitor who has not yet thought of this, then your product is in danger of becoming obsolete. But if you are a tire distributor or retailer, you face an existential threat. As tire manufacturers sell and deliver directly, distributors and retailers will become irrelevant. Neither tire manufacturers nor customers will need them, and they will face elimination from the industry value chain. This illustrates how businesses must blend technology into value propositions and business models.

Basic information is available through a number of sources—customer behavior and technology trends affecting products and services—and must be studied at a detailed level through research and data collection. However, keeping track of customer behavior and technology is barely enough to understand the full picture. There are several more hard-to-see dynamics hiding beneath the surface of the Digital Faultline.

Force 3—Global Competition: Innovation Can Begin Anywhere

We tend to assume that only large, resource-rich companies with well-funded R&D organizations can lead in innovation. We also think that countries with well-established educational systems, strong research capabilities, and big economies will lead in innovation. This will not be the case moving forward.

Every innovation begins with the purpose of addressing an existing or new consumer or human need. In many parts of the world, these needs are still quite basic, such as access to food, water, electricity, education, healthcare, and safety. The fewer resources a region or a community has, the harder it is for people to gain sustained access to these necessities. Enter digitalization.

With the availability of wireless internet, online education and knowledge are easily accessible around the world. US and European universities now offer online education to students globally. Similarly, "how-to" kits in any field are available online. Over the years, the advantage of developed nations and established companies has eroded. They no longer have a monopoly on the building blocks that underpin solutions to a human need.

Access to knowledge makes the world a much smaller place as far as innovation is concerned. Within the less-developed regions of the world are shining jewels of human endeavor, creativity, and entrepreneurship. What is common about them is their intense focus on solving a basic human need. Some of them are future competitors of established players.

Table 1 below shows innovations from locations far away from the known hubs of innovation such as Silicon Valley or Bangalore or Seoul.

Necessity is still the mother of invention. Innovation will occur anywhere and everywhere in the world so long as human needs remain unfulfilled. Local innovators will develop solutions at prices people in that part of the world can afford.

Though unstructured and poorly resourced, the power of this innovation lies in the fervent beliefs of its pursuers, the simplicity of their designs, and absence of organizational constraints. These teams of "village" innovators do not need vast resources. They are not bound by legacy investments, organizational politics, or bureaucratic approval processes. They overcome roadblocks and far exceed the speed of execution by large companies.

Successful ideas and innovations eventually receive financial support from various organizations. These could be governments, social investors, and nonprofits such as UNICEF, the World Health Organization, or the Gates Foundation. Large forward-thinking corporations and venture capitalists invest too. When the right sponsor provides capital and management expertise to a ripe idea even in an underdeveloped region, it acquires the scalability of a Silicon Valley start-up.

A final consideration to keep in mind: developing countries are also advancing their own intellectual property-protection frameworks. Their goal is to ensure that innovations created in their respective countries stay in their countries, creating the expected social and economic benefits and advantages.

Incumbent companies can no longer control innovation with their financial resources alone. They must systematically track innovation, which can occur anywhere in the world. It can arrive at any industry at any time with a disruptive force and turn existing value propositions on their heads.

TABLE 1. EXAMPLES OF INNOVATION ARISING FAR FROM TRADITIONAL HUBS

	COUNTRY	HUMAN NEED	COMPANY	PRODUCT	INDUSTRY
	Argentina	Small-to-medium businesses easily connecting with customers	Cliengo	AI-assisted chatbot	
	Argentina, Brazil, Colombia	Supporting local entrepreneurs via blockchain technology	NEM	Smart asset company aiding blockchain developments in LATAM	
	Togo	Reducing electronic waste	WoeLab	3D printers built from local e-waste	
	Nigeria	Affordable, accessible digital payments for the unbanked	Kudi	Online payments platform and network of agents converting cash into/from digital payments	
	Uganda	Reducing infant and mother mortality	Teheca	App that links healthcare practitioners/caregivers to mothers online and offline	
	Cameroon	Optimizing agricultural yields and reducing costs	Will & Brothers	Precision farming using drones	

	COUNTRY	HUMAN NEED	COMPANY	PRODUCT	INDUSTRY
	Kazakhstan	Rehabilitating patients after stroke	ReLive	AI-powered exoskeleton used to retrain mind-muscle connections	
	Kazakhstan	Reducing mill shutdowns due to power overloads	Eurasian Resources Group	Digital/smart mining	
	Turkmenistan	Simple and affordable cashless payments using mobile phones	Rysgal Bank	QR code for payments	
	Pakistan	Female doctors in underserved communities	Sehat Kahani	Mobile-based telehealth solution	
	India	Allowing programmers to code in peace— anywhere, anytime	Dcoder	Mobile coding platform	

© Trianz 2020

Force 4—From Global Markets to Global Competition: Asia Now Leads in Product Development

The age of globalization began with trade and commerce treaties that took shape in the 1970s, 1980s, and 1990s. Regions with large populations and an emerging middle class, such as China, India, and parts of the Middle East and Africa, became great export markets for the West. Over time, the scope of trade expanded from exporting goods and services to local manufacturing and distribution within the region. We are now transitioning from these regions simply being markets for the West to them becoming a source of global competition that, in many cases, is taking the lead over Western competitors.

Within the well-organized corporate sectors of the world, we tend to assume that the United States and Western Europe have a monopoly or a large lead in introducing new products and services to the market. That is no longer the case. Asia-Pacific has emerged as the leader in both the pace of innovation and new product/service launches (TGTS data; see Figure 2).

FIGURE 2. TIME TO MARKET FOR NEW PRODUCT LAUNCH

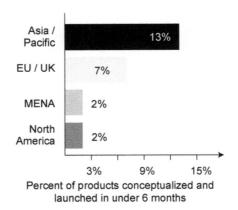

© Trianz Research (Trasers) 2021

One in seven products in Asia is launched within six months or less. While this varies by industry, it is important to note that Asia has an 11 percent time to market lead over North America and a 6 percent lead over the EU in this category.

What is powering Asia's acceleration and emerging technological independence?

First, Asia saw decades of investment by Western companies seeking new markets. This created jobs, uplifted local economies, and improved household incomes. The need for more blue-collar and white-collar talent created an increasing emphasis on education in these countries. Government incentives encouraged the creation

> Asia-Pacific has emerged as the leader in both the pace of innovation and new product/service launches. One in seven products in Asia is launched within six months or less.

of indigenous technology and homegrown entrepreneurship. All this converged to create local companies enabled by educational systems and well-trained workforces. For every Ford and GE, there is a Tata and Mahindra in India. For every Boeing or Airbus, there is now a COMAC in China, and so on. From humble origins as suppliers for Western companies, these companies have now grown into international players.

The second big reason for Asia's emergence is the role that a massive local population plays for regional companies. Half of the world's 7.2 billion people live in just seven countries: China, India, Indonesia, Pakistan, Bangladesh, the Philippines, and Vietnam. This affords a unique opportunity for local companies. They have a better understanding of the local populations and can deliver products and services similar to global companies but at lower costs. They adapt to local customer-product interactions and feedback loops faster than their global rivals. For example, based on its knowledge of low incomes and price sensitivity, Indian conglomerate Reliance recently launched a new telecom brand called Jio. Within a year, Jio changed the communications industry in India, eroding the profits of all its rivals and taking over market leadership.

The third major factor is the "leapfrog effect." Western nations have evolved sequentially from one generation of technology infrastructure to another. For example, in telecommunications and the internet, the West has gone from telegraph and PABX-based landlines to Voice over Internet Protocol (VoIP), satellite, and wireless networks. The challenge for companies in the West is that they still have legacy infrastructures with large residual value. Consequently, these companies can adopt new technologies only at a pace their financials can absorb. These financial dynamics slow down modernization, impacting development cycles and time to market. But in the Digital Age, velocity is everything.

Asian companies, on the other hand, do not have to worry about winding down past investments or protecting legacy products. They skip straight to new technologies and accelerate compared with their Western counterparts. Thus begins a cycle that impacts their business models, customers, revenues, costs, and profits. As profits scale, the ability of local competitors to invest improves quickly compared with Western companies.

The point behind the Asian innovation story is that Western companies can no longer view the Middle East, China, India, and all of Asia as export markets. Companies in these regions innovate at a pace faster than do their Western multinationals. We have evolved from an age of global markets to an age of global technology competition.

Established companies in Western economies can no longer treat Asian counterparts as imitators or cheaper alternatives. These are now legitimate international competitors capable of structured and scalable innovation.

Force 5—Many Davids vs. a Few Goliaths: The Rise of Upstarts

Large companies or "Goliaths" tend to compare themselves to known peers and rivals in the industry. We tend to think of Pfizer vs. Merck, GM vs. Toyota, Coke vs. Pepsi, Shell vs. Chevron, P&G vs. Unilever, GE vs. ABB, and so on. However, competition on the Digital Faultline is not only from known players or Asia but also from numerous unknown "Davids," start-ups from within the industry or from tech.

The very word "start-up" traces its origins to the tech industry and Silicon Valley. Until a decade or so ago, such start-ups were common only to the tech industry. Their scope was also limited to producing new software (SW), hardware (HW), semiconductors, networking equipment, and video games. Some, such as PayPal and eBay, ventured into e-businesses. Entrepreneurial managers with a vision for something new or better would break away from larger tech companies and start as "garage operations." This literally meant starting from the garage in someone's house or a small office. For example, Hewlett Packard really started from a garage in Palo Alto. Steve Jobs and Steve Wozniak originally started what became Apple from Jobs's parents' garage in California. Such start-ups would reach a "minimum viable product" and then make a pitch to venture capitalists or private equity firms, which would then invest. Some of these companies scaled very quickly with the rest of the organizational capabilities falling into place as they grew. Access to enormous amounts of capital and, later, their own cash flows would ensure that capital was never a problem for those start-ups.

In the past decade, the start-up phenomenon has spread from tech to every industry globally. The pattern of teaming, proving a tech-based concept and business model, gaining access to funding, and scaling is identical to that of Silicon Valley start-ups. Worldwide start-up investments reached about $300 billion in 2019—along with that, the number of Davids in any industry has also grown exponentially.

But how is the ancient story of David vs. Goliath relevant here? While the fight between a young boy named David and a terrifying giant named Goliath is portrayed as one of great courage, it also involved determination and a unique skill. The act of David volunteering to fight Goliath shows the dimension of courage and determination in wanting to protect his people. What is less known is that David was an exceptional slinger, a specialized foot soldier who had been trained to fight enemies with a slingshot. A sling is a leather pouch attached to a cord that cradles a stone. After spinning it rapidly in a rotating motion, slingers would hurl the stone toward their target with deadly accuracy. The velocity and force of the stone would often end up being fatal for the target. In the fight, David managed to hit Goliath in the forehead. Goliath fell with a thud, killed instantly by the stone from the sling. The army accompanying Goliath conceded the battle, and David's people lived to fight another day.

The challenge for large companies on the Digital Faultline is that not one but many Davids are arising in every industry at the same time. Each of these Davids brings courage, a fanatical customer centricity, a technology-based solution, and special techniques to deliver value. They have the courage to start a business in spaces dominated by industry giants and the determination to

> The challenge for large companies on the Digital Faultline is that not one but many Davids are arising in every industry at the same time.

overcome any obstacles. They refine their tech-centric value proposition iteratively and ultimately achieve success. As soon as there is any evidence of customer adoption of a product or service, investors swoop in with large capital to bolster the nascent company. And thus they begin to compete with established companies at scale. This neutralizes the market power of Goliaths, as Davids move rapidly before larger companies even blink.

To defeat a large incumbent's product or service, not every David in an industry needs to win. It only takes one or two Davids to scale to topple giant companies and transform industries. Just ask Yellow Pages about Google, Sears about Amazon, Blockbuster and AMC Cinemas about Netflix, and the auto industry about Tesla.

Force 6—Encroachment by the Tech Industry

As is now well known, the tech industry has successfully encroached on other industries since the early 2000s. It has sometimes carved out significant market shares or turned business models in an entire industry upside down. There are many popular examples—Amazon in retail, Netflix in entertainment, Microsoft in travel (Expedia) and entertainment (Xbox), Apple in communications and entertainment, PayPal in payment processing, eBay in the auction business, and so on.

This encroachment thus far has mostly been in transactional and easy-to-understand consumer markets, where tech companies either deliver the same value in a more efficient manner or render existing value propositions obsolete. In the next wave, hi-tech will be launching businesses in areas where problems are larger and yet to be solved. And they will bring their hallmark tech-driven approach to solving these problems. Technologies such as artificial intelligence (AI), augmented or virtual reality (AR or VR), robotics, etc., will accelerate solutions. Here are a few simple examples of hi-tech in action:

Using analytics and algorithms, tech companies are beginning to report breakthroughs in early breast cancer detections. If their approach works, it has the potential to make cancer-detection equipment providers obsolete.

In mining, SpaceX is working toward minimizing the effects of mining on the planet. Having successfully developed reusable rockets, SpaceX's next goal is to land on asteroids that carry minerals in huge volumes. The idea is to mine at scale and reduce damage to the Earth's already fragile environment and climate.

In home security, Ring has built the virtual lock. Using cameras and connected apps, users can open doors remotely while watching who comes in. Ring has affected the "lock and key" and the home security industries simultaneously with this solution.

Heal is changing primary healthcare. Patients can use their service, which is now accepted by major US insurers, to schedule a doctor's visit at home. This obviously is convenient for patients, but it also helps primary care doctors to better manage patient care.

These are just some easy-to-understand examples. However, there are countless such models being developed at any given point in time by large tech or small start-ups. Each one approaches human or business needs or opportunities that can be solved through technology. The companies do not care about existing industry players or structures but are intently focused on innovation and proving the concept. By the time established companies in an industry see the product or service, it is too late. Disruption has already taken place.

Catalyzed even more by the COVID-19 pandemic, hi-tech will encroach wherever it can. That process begins by taking a data-driven approach to understanding a problem and developing multiple tech-centric solution alternatives. As soon as an approach clicks, the company builds momentum and is in a space occupied by an incumbent even before the latter realizes the threat.

The Sum Total of the Forces on the Faultline

While each of the six forces have been described individually in this chapter, they are not isolated from each other when they act. Similar to the forces in an earthquake, they act in tandem with each other. For example, global innovation and many Davids can come together to create disruptive competition from anywhere in the world. Similarly, customers and digital technologies can come together for purchasing products or services from anywhere. Geographic boundaries and market leverage of large, established incumbents will not be able to stop these trends.

It will take time and even more data for us to understand these and other forces in a more structured manner. In the short term, their destructive effects will be unpredictable and have differing consequences. These may be severe in certain industries, such as retail, wearables, etc., which are easy to disrupt. It may be less severe in other industries that are highly regulated and capital intensive, such as energy and utilities.

What we can be sure of is that in the long term, no industry will be left untouched by changing customer behavior, digital technologies, start-ups, global innovation, Asian competitors, and encroachment by hi-tech. What we can also be sure of is that no incumbent company or country can control any of these forces—let alone all of them.

Therefore, instead of either ignoring or consuming energy in trying to control these forces, business leaders must first regain control over their own situation. Instead of building grand five-year visions and strategies, as was done in the past, leaders must now focus on getting to a place of safety and control over fundamentals. That is what *Crossing the Digital Faultline* is all about.

Once they cross the faultline, lay strong foundations, and have enough data about their specific situation, they will be able to see how these forces are impacting their industry and business context. They will then evolve to the next stage, similar to tae kwon do, wherein they begin to utilize these outside forces to fully transform their business and gain sustainable competitive advantage.

CHAPTER 3

DIGITAL, DIGITAL TRANSFORMATION, AND BUSINESS TRANSFORMATION

Digital Transformation: What Is It Anyway?

Until now, there has been no basic or standardized definition of "digital transformation," which has led to a great deal of confusion. Do a quick internet search, and you will see the words "digital," "digitalization," and "digital transformation" used freely and interchangeably with endless variations in meaning. Every article will have technology soundbites and "expert" opinions but no expert agrees with another.

This lack of standardized definitions and a major gap in understanding of fundamentals has caused a chaotic misalignment among leaders. This often takes place within the same company faced with cascading confusion in various functional or IT teams.

In the Trianz Global Transformation Survey (TGTS), we wanted to see how leaders perceived the digital trends happening all around us and how they were coping with the urgency for pursuing necessary transformation. In fact, the very first question we asked in our surveys was, "What does digital transformation mean to you?"

While we had anticipated that some percentage of respondents might not understand the term, the results were shocking: 51 percent of worldwide business and IT leaders from across twenty different industries thought of digital transformation as merely upgrading to new websites or online portals.

Only 5 percent of more than ten thousand respondents truly understood the true meaning of digital transformation, which is "truly understanding customer behavior, reimagining products and services, and delivering high-velocity, digitalized experiences across the value chain to all stakeholders—even if it calls for discarding existing models."

These percentages have changed significantly post-COVID—but that still raises the question: why do a large percentage of industry leaders think "digital" refers primarily to websites? After the rollout of the public internet in the early 1990s, the first generation of technology innovations included browsers, websites, email, e-commerce, VoIP networks, pagers, mobile phones, video sharing, SMS, and text messaging. The "digital" label became popular in marketing circles in the mid-2000s, but at the time it meant cool websites.

Over time, internet, e-commerce, and mobile phone usage converged to create tectonic shifts in consumer behavior. An increasing number of companies launched great-looking websites with digital versions of their product catalog ready for customers to peruse at their leisure. Online product and service reviews became instantly available in every industry, empowering consumers to make decisions based on the collective feedback of people they had never met. The look and feel of products and services, utility in favor of brand, the convenience of online shopping, reviews, likes, and shares (the digital version of word of mouth) all started to gain prominence. Collectively, these things brought about a new digital era—one in which products and services were being purchased online instead of in retail stores.

Except for a few smart companies that understood and holistically prepared for this shift, marketing efforts in most organizations focused on rebranding the company and its products and services to raise awareness and appeal for this new wave of consumers. This was generally without regard for whether the underlying value proposition had changed. Today, rebranding of companies and creating cool websites are still important, but they merely signify the very first stage of a company's evolution. Things have moved far beyond that mark.

Since the 2000s, continued technological advances and innovations across all industries have received a great deal of attention, but a key statistic has gone mostly unnoticed across the business universe: the average age of a first-time phone user or owner has now dropped to ten or eleven years worldwide. As an extension, we know that more than 90 percent of children between the ages of two and seventeen in developed nations (such as the United States, Japan, Korea, UK, and big parts of Europe) play video games mostly over the internet. Join the two and you will see profound implications for all businesses: we have reached the point where human beings are born with phones. By the time these children grow to be adults (i.e., when they become your prospective customers), their behaviors, values, needs, and preferences have already been set. What they see, what they read, how they evaluate, how much time they have, what they are willing to pay, and above all, the relative importance of a product and what they value within the product will be vastly different from generation to generation. The most critical thing leaders must understand about transformations is that they are not generic: every organization must better understand customer behavior within the context of their industry's specific products or services.

Therefore, digital transformation is the reimagination of your company's product or service value propositions and the underlying business value chain to deliver highly digitalized experiences to customers and all stakeholders, 24/7, 365 days a year.

It is equally important for us to know what digital transformation is not. Contrary to the buzz and the blatant marketing, technology is not a goal in and of itself. It is simply a vehicle to deliver value, new propositions, and experiences. The most successful companies in our surveys, our Digital Champions, focus on business outcomes. None of them began their transformation process by focusing on technology. However, they did apply it aggressively and successfully to achieve measurable outcomes. I will elaborate on the role of technology in transformations as we get to the 10 Rules.

> Contrary to the buzz and the blatant marketing, technology is not a goal in and of itself. It is simply a vehicle to deliver value, new propositions, and experiences.

The Difference between Digital and Business Transformation

Transformations do not happen overnight, and successful leaders know this. They research their customers, technologies, and competitors to invent or upgrade value propositions. The longer a company or a product or service has been in existence, the more time it will take to change. Whether a team succeeds or fails in the first iteration, its future iterations will succeed, provided it makes the right adjustments. For example, the second generation of iPhone, Tesla, GoPro, and

Alexa were very different (and better) than the first releases. Similarly, their third releases were better than the second. Conversely, those who do not understand, do not commit to action, or do not reinvent themselves successfully will perish.

Companies that sustain their efforts will see new value propositions being accepted by customers. As they continue their commitment, they discover completely new ways of engaging customers and delivering experiences. The more an organization analyzes underlying data, the more ideas it will generate for new value propositions. Along the way, leadership, employees, technology competence, decision-making, and value chains also transform. With new ideas emerging once every few iterations, new ventures and business units get created. That is when the cycle of business transformation begins.

Few companies are succeeding in digital transformation today. Fewer still are conscious about the new opportunities that emerge because of early iterations and continuous data analysis, and even fewer pursue them. The ones who take the bold steps to pursue those new opportunities, which are often not in their current business, will see nonlinear growth flying up the curve of success. Consequently, their new business will become larger than the traditional business. At some point, their new employees, customers, and partners may not even know what the company used to be. That is when business transformation will have occurred.

Let us bring this concept of "business transformation" to life with two of the most recognizable companies—Apple and Amazon (Figure 3). Both have been through numerous cycles of change and continue to evolve at a rapid pace even while being leaders in their industries.

Steve Jobs returned in 1992 to an Apple that was struggling. It was a company with a declining personal computer business in near-fatal financial condition. There were other challenges besides becoming irrelevant in the PC industry. In exchange for making the Microsoft Office suite available, Microsoft had made Internet Explorer mandatory on Apple PCs. In retaliation, Apple sued Microsoft under antitrust laws, even as it was dependent on Microsoft. The only thing Apple had going for it was an iconic brand and a cult-like following among its customers.

One of the first things Jobs did upon rejoining Apple was to reach an agreement with Microsoft founder Bill Gates. In a joint interview with Gates, Jobs famously said, "Our realization was that for Apple to win, Microsoft did not have to lose, or vice versa." Microsoft invested $150 million in Apple and would continue making products for Apple. In exchange, Apple dropped its lawsuit against Microsoft.

Jobs then focused on Apple's business portfolio. In the first phase of reinventing Apple, he reimagined the Macintosh computer, which became the iconic iMac. He then introduced the iPod, iPad, and iTunes. Jobs's obsession with launching innovative products is legendary. What Apple was really doing was reinventing its customer experiences and rapidly getting into new businesses.

Within a decade, Apple had launched several new products such as the iPhone, Apple Watch, Apple TV+, Apple Pay, and the Apple credit card. Through these transformations, Apple became a consumer electronics, credit card, and entertainment company. It had long left behind its traditional rivals in the PC business. It also began beating competitors across the electronics, watch, and music industries. Apple's business had transformed—PCs, its original business, now contributes less than 10 percent of its $200B plus annual revenues.

Similarly, Jeff Bezos founded Amazon as an online store for buying and selling used books. In the 2000s, Amazon entered general online retail, and today it sells every consumer product imaginable on the planet. The company also sells cloud technologies to businesses (and the US government) and has its own grocery chain in the form of the Whole Foods store. It produces and delivers its own entertainment content via Amazon Prime, its distribution channel. Amazon's original used-books business is now less than 5 percent of its overall revenues. Amazon has now transformed to a point where new employees and customers may no longer know what the company's original core business was.

Microsoft, Apple, Amazon, and Alphabet (Google) are less than forty-five years old and are the top five companies in the world by market capitalization. It is a misnomer to still call them "technology businesses." In reality, they have transformed into conglomerates where their original businesses are just a small part of who they are today (Figure 3). They transform by understanding their consumers and enterprise customers. They transform by digitalizing their businesses and providing great experiences. They systematically collect data and expand of their portfolios and entering new businesses. They are never satisfied, and they do not pause or stop.

FIGURE 3. EXAMPLES OF BUSINESS TRANSFORMATION

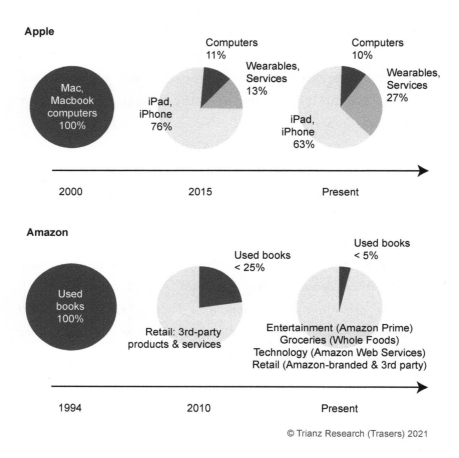

© Trianz Research (Trasers) 2021

"Digital" is about cool sites and apps, and "digital transformation" is the process of reimagining product/service value propositions and reinventing value chains into experience chains.

"Business transformation" is the continuous reimagination and expansion of product/service portfolios and technologies and evolution of leadership, talent, decision-making, digitalization of the value chain, and organizational culture—to a point where the business no longer resembles its original form.

CHAPTER 4

WINDOWS OF OPPORTUNITY OR WINDOWS OF CRISIS

The Accelerating Pace of Change on the Faultline

The notion that we are in the "second industrial revolution" is a cliché. What is unique, however, is the scale and rate of change. Let us take a closer look to better understand the notion of pace in this digital age. The first industrial revolution began in the 1760s with the invention of steam-powered spinning machines. The automated motion of spindles increased textile mill output by forty times. A remarkable century of inventions and discoveries transformed businesses, societies, and human life. But the term "industrial revolution" was only coined decades later because the change did not *begin* on an industrial scale. In fact, it was not even known to the world beyond Britain for a long time. It took more than 150 for the change to be felt at a global scale.

The twentieth century saw the invention of seemingly impossible and paradigm-changing creations, such as electricity, petroleum, automobiles, air travel, television, communications, etc. These were propagated around the world within a decade or two at most. From there, the rate of change accelerated exponentially.

The pace of change across industries began picking up speed in the PC era of the 1990s and 2000s with technology-led inventions (tablet computers, the internet, mobile phones, apps, video, social media) and the emergence of new fields (alternative energy, genomics, digital entertainment, digital health, etc.). It took 150 years for the first industrial revolution to achieve global scale. The application of new technologies and business paradigms is simultaneous in this second revolution. What is launched in Silicon Valley reaches Bangalore, Kuala Lumpur, or Johannesburg instantaneously.

This pace of change will now accelerate with breathtaking speed across all industries globally. As knowledge bases become globally available, technical skills proliferate quickly. Components required to build complex solutions are sold globally. It means that what is available to Verizon in the US is available to Deutsche Telecom in EU but also to AirTel in India or Singtel in Singapore. Such dynamics lead to global competition and shrinking innovation cycles across industries. Let us look at some examples of shrinking time frames.

> It took 150 years for the first industrial revolution to achieve global scale. The application of new technologies and business paradigms is simultaneous in this second revolution. What is launched in Silicon Valley reaches Bangalore, Kuala Lumpur, or Johannesburg instantaneously.

New product cycles take eighteen to twenty-four months across industries, while revamping existing products takes less than one year. In industries that used to take years to roll out new products, both of these are historic lows. A movie made by Disney in the US or an enhancement to the Disney+ platform can be implemented within days and weeks around the world. Even the converse can be true, given that Asia leads in product-development cycles.

New products, services, and innovation could originate in Asia first and be introduced into the US or EU. Samsung is from Korea, Flipkart is from India, Sony is from Japan, and so on. Change is therefore not just faster but can come from any direction and become global instantly.

We can measure how much a company has digitalized or the pace at which an industry is being transformed by aggregating data. In the TGTS research, we analyzed data on current states, new business models, processes, use of digital technologies, and organizational change. While many factors contribute, the two that make transformations real are analytics and business process digitalization. Analytics influence strategy and prioritization and predicts outcomes; process or business model digitalization changes the definition of value and stakeholder experiences.

Figure 4 below shows the positioning of eighteen industries studied by TGTS on these two dimensions. The first chart shows the state of industries in 2018, and the second chart shows the expected positioning of industries in 2020.

The y-axis of Figure 4 describes the level of industry digitization from low to high while the x-axis describes the level of data analytics from low to high. In 2018, hi-tech, banking, and telecom had advanced into the visionary quadrant (high process digitization and high state of analytics). This is the quadrant of visionaries where analytics guide the digitalization agenda. On the bottom left (low digitization and low analytics) were slow-moving, highly regulated, and concentrated industries. They either did not feel the incentive to change or were constrained but remained as-is.

FIGURE 4. CHANGE STATE OF DIGITAL TRANSFORMATION WORLDWIDE
ACROSS INDUSTRIES

State of Transformations Worldwide: 2019

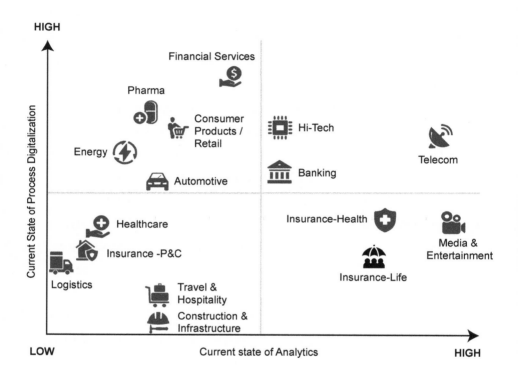

Estimated State of Transformations Worldwide: 2022

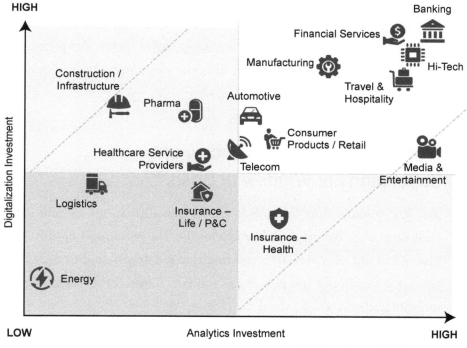

© Trianz Research (Trasers) 2021

The 2020 data show how industry positions shift based on their investments into analytics and process digitalization. We now have more players in the top-right (visionary) quadrant. More importantly—*all* industries are now in a directionally aligned band and getting out of the state of inertia. The 2020 data should not be misunderstood to somehow depict an end state where all industries converge to the top right. Rather, the entire matrix is moving to the top right, and what is visionary today will be status quo tomorrow. In effect, it is a continuous, nonstop digital race within and across industries.

The forces on the faultline will act more in concert with each other. When one force succeeds and catalyzes certain variables, other forces feed on it and create their own impact. The connection between customer behavior, technology, start-ups, and global innovation shape chain reactions. These forces will crash into each other, creating a rupturing effect and changing an industry's fundamentals forever. As an overall consequence of this convergence of forces, the pace of this disruption will only increase. This means competitive cycles or windows will become shorter and shorter.

What Is Your Choice—Window of Opportunity or Window of Crisis?

The key message thus far is this: digital transformations are still in their early stage but are rapidly accelerating. The window of opportunity is still open for the large and traditional enterprise—but only if you act scientifically and before it is too late. Consider the following insights from the TGTS data:

Fewer than 30 percent of leaders in R&D are confident about their product and service portfolio. Nearly half think their competitors are innovating faster.

Fewer than 25 percent of processes across the business value chain in all industries have been digitalized.

Fewer than 30 percent of companies have invested adequately into analytics. This is changing and analytics will be the number one technology investment by CIOs in the next several years.

Cloud adoption is in the early stages in all industries except for hi-tech, entertainment, financial services, and travel. But more than 50 percent of companies expect to make the cloud the default for development of new products, services, and business applications.

The biggest impact of the cloud is not only cost reduction but also an acceleration of the product-service development cycles.

In every industry, rethinking of products, services, and digitalizing value chains will clearly accelerate. As this change crosses a tipping point, the face of that industry will begin to change. We have seen how entertainment has moved from the big screen to smart devices. COVID has shown how education has moved from the classroom to online, investing has now moved from the brokerage office to a phone app, and so on.

While the window of opportunity to change varies by industry, it will shrink rapidly until it becomes a window of crisis for slow movers. Innovators in the industry will accelerate, and new entrants will emerge from outside the industry with even more cutting-edge value propositions. But when a company faces a window of crisis, it is likely too late.

What are the choices your company and, by extension, you as a leader have in today's dynamic environment? Let us use the framework below to understand how a team either leads or falls fatally behind. The x-axis of Figure 5 describes the pace of industry change from slow to fast, while the y-axis describes the competitive position of a company. To make it interesting, plot your company in the appropriate quadrant.

FIGURE 5. TRANSFORMATION QUADRANT AND COMPETITIVE CHOICES

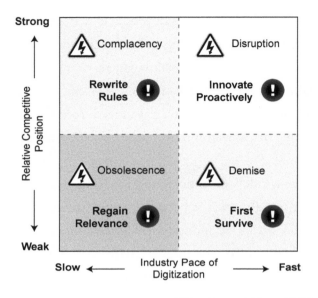

© Trianz Research (Trasers) 2021

Now, let us understand what each quadrant means and the choices of a player in any one of these quadrants.

- **Weak Company in a Slow-Paced Industry (Lower-Left Quadrant).** This company must innovate faster than its industry or face obsolescence in the industry due to encroachment by tech and start-ups. Its first task is to survive by regaining relevance with customers by innovating on today's paradigms. Examples: energy, education, arts, healthcare, insurance.

- **Weak Company in a Fast-Paced Industry (Lower-Right Quadrant).** Here, the company faces enormous risk from faster and innovative start-ups as well as established companies. This company's first task is to ensure its own survival by innovating more rapidly than the industry average and scaling quickly. Examples: consumer products, banking, semiconductors, tech.

- **Strong Company in a Slow-Paced Industry (Upper-Left Quadrant).** While the company itself may be in a dominant position, the entire industry or key value propositions could be disrupted by start-ups or tech. It must avoid complacency and rewrite the rules of its current business, perhaps even venturing into new space as it begins to succeed. Example: energy, automotive, healthcare, and insurance.

- **Strong Company in a Fast-Paced Industry (Upper-Right Quadrant).** A large company in this quadrant cannot become complacent, as it faces the highest risk of being disrupted. Either its known competitors are changing rapidly or new start-up and tech competitors are emerging with new value propositions. Its task is to innovate proactively to maintain its competitive position.

What you see in this analysis is a rare occurrence. No matter the current competitive position and no matter whether the industry is fast or slow, companies and their leaders have one only choice. That choice is to innovate quickly, maintain or regain relevance, and grow from there.

Leaders who choose aggressive innovation, imagine new value propositions, and execute rapidly will see the Digital Age as a window of immense opportunity. Those who are complacent, wish change away, remain ignorant, afraid, and overly cautious, or flat-out blame their challenges on everything except their own inaction will soon face a window of existential crisis.

Once a company enters a window of crisis, the probability of its survival is low. The forces of change from within and outside the industry will have turned into a tornado that cannot be combated. The time will simply have passed, its resources would have been depleted, and its best talent may have left the company. TGTS data shows that 30 percent of companies across industries that demonstrate this type of behavior will become obsolete by or before 2030 (TGTS data). This is a choice that leaders must make—or it will be made for them. Their companies will either innovate and transition into the Digital Age or perish with their market share gobbled up by innovators within or from outside their industry.

Companies that do break loose from the present uncertainties will see an evolution of their products and services, higher acceptance levels by customers, better productivity across the value chain, and a general sense of how to move forward. Let us look at this evolutionary process.

CHAPTER 5

STAGES OF EVOLUTION AND DIGITAL CHAMPION COMPANIES

The transformation journey begins by developing a shared understanding of digitalization among an organization's leadership. From there, individual leaders must develop a data-driven vision, make the tough decisions, and set priorities for their respective areas of responsibility. In some cases, centralized roles (such the COO, chief data or digital officer) may unify initiatives under one umbrella and arrive at similar decisions. Finally, they must marshal the necessary people and financial resources to execute their visions. When a team does begin executing, it may see few or no benefits in the early stages. But perseverance is key.

Depending on the industry and the company's size, it may take up to two years for key performance indicators (KPIs) to show a clear transition away from the Digital Faultline. KPIs are metrics that tell us how key elements of a product, service, business model, process, application, or audience are trending. Lagging KPIs tell you about what has already happened, and leading KPIs indicate what will most likely happen.

So how will this evolution take place, and how can you identify where your company is in the process?

Stages of Evolution on the Digital Faultline

Using the TGTS data, we developed the Trianz Digital Enterprise Evolution Model (Figure 6) to illustrate the different stages of digital maturity of a company or a business within a given industry context.

FIGURE 6. TRIANZ DIGITAL ENTERPRISE EVOLUTION MODEL (DEEM)©

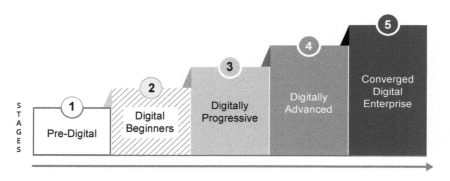

© Trianz Research (Trasers) 2021

Each level is an aggregate of the maturity of the underlying products, services, business models, processes, operations, IT infrastructure, and talent. The five stages of evolution in the model can be described as follows:

- **Stage 1—Pre-Digital:** Companies that have yet to begin transformation.

- **Stage 2—Digital Beginners:** Companies that are still in legacy models but may have begun their journey.

- **Stage 3—Digitally Progressive:** Companies already committed to the transition. They have made changes to products, digitalized 40–50 percent of processes, and built various other capabilities.

- **Stage 4—Digitally Advanced:** Companies that have transformed most of their products, services, and operations. Their technology foundation is solid, and they heavily use predictive analytics.

- **Stage 5—Converged Digital Enterprise:** Companies that make data-driven decisions across all levels. Their visions and priorities evolve by predicting customer behavior. They do business digitally everywhere possible. These companies have a sharp, well-aligned, and high-digital-IQ leadership. They also have well-trained talent, digital workplaces, and modern, global cultures. In effect, every aspect of their business has converged to data, customers, technologies, and a digital way of doing things.

Amazon, Microsoft, Apple, Google, Tesla, Lyft, Uber, Facebook, Twitter, Walmart, Disney+, Square, 23andMe, Netflix, and Adobe are examples of digitally converged enterprises. Each of them is in an industry such as retail, entertainment, health, and social media. At the same time, they also call themselves and behave as technology companies. Companies in this group will evolve faster and reshape their industries. They will demonstrate breakthrough financial performance and will eventually grow into new areas. Ultimately, they may change to a point where they may not resemble who they are today. These are the companies that will excel in the Digital Age.

In contrast, there are once-great brand names that disconnected from their customers over time and stagnated. They did not realize that change was even happening—or worse, did absolutely nothing about that change or wished it away. These companies eventually perished or lost market share to a point where they are no longer relevant in their industries. Kodak, Polaroid, Blockbuster, Sears Roebuck & Co., Borders, Toys "R" Us, HMV, Macy's, and Radio Shack are examples in this category. Nor is the tech industry immune to this phenomenon. The repercussions of falling behind in the race are quite brutal in an industry that is ultra-Darwinian. Netscape, Nokia, Toshiba, Yahoo, Blackberry, AOL, and Nortel Networks are examples of pioneering brands that are no longer relevant.

Measuring a Company's Digital Maturity and Competitiveness

How do we determine the competitiveness of a company? Experts in the traditional model cite brand, R&D, manufacturing, sales and distribution, management, growth rate, and financial strength as key factors. When we study the demise of established companies and the success of start-ups in the tech industry, a different story begins to emerge. TGTS shows that many of these factors do not play a material role in the evolution, growth, and performance of a company in the Digital Age.

Data shows that the following five factors determine the digital competitiveness of a company or a business function:

The "Digital IQ" of a Company's Leadership

A shared understanding of industry change, alignment on their own digital vision, and synchronized execution by its leadership are the fundamental requirements. The more the leadership team utilizes data for decision-making, the more likely the company is to succeed. Conversely, it does not matter how much capital a company spends; unless its leadership has a high Digital IQ it will not succeed. Digital IQ is the fundamental and essential component through which all other success factors come to life.

The Relevance of the Company's Product/Service Portfolio

As discussed earlier, customers in every B2B and B2C industry are changing. The success of a company's new value propositions will begin to show in top-line growth, customer retention, and referrals. It means that customers are accepting the company's new value propositions. The more this happens, the more likely their transformation will gain momentum.

The Degree of Digitalization of the Company's Business Processes

Delivering high-velocity, connected, and low-touch experiences for all stakeholders is key. Digital processes between customers, partners, suppliers, regulators, leadership, and employees drive productivity and velocity. Besides enabling the new value promise, digitalized processes are important and continuous sources of data. This data can be harnessed to iterate every aspect of the business.

The Readiness of the Company's Talent and Its Organizational Culture

The better a company's talent is trained to handle technology-enabled processes, the faster the company will evolve. The more modern, global, open, and communicative the culture, the faster it will adapt to digital paradigms. TGTS data shows that role-based training on new processes is the number one predictor of success of transformational initiatives.

The Preparedness of the Company's Cybersecurity Function

Readers may be surprised to see security mentioned as a critical factor. It is to be noted that cybercrime is accelerating several times faster than businesses are transforming. In other words, the bad guys have changed their business model already. As processes become digital, user data, customers, financials, and IP are exposed to cybercriminals. The financial liabilities and brand damage due to data breaches are enormous. In addition, regulations will soon be expanding to address this threat in all industries. Companies will simply not be able to launch new products, services, or processes that are not security compliant. Therefore, security can either be the unsung hero or the maligned villain in the Digital Age.

These five factors combine to form what we call the "digital competitiveness" of a company, which grows over time. It is competitive because the sooner you begin to appeal to customers, the sooner you begin succeeding. The sooner you analyze data from your success, the sooner you will frame your next iteration. And this triangulation sets the compass direction and the speed at which to drive. Before beginning this transitional journey, it is critical for companies to know how they fare against peers and leaders in their industry.

The simple quiz that follows will help you to identify your company's (or business function's) stage of digital maturity at a high level. In the self-assessment, "leadership" refers to the top management at a company or business/IT function level. In the case of a company, "customers" (marked with an asterisk in the quiz) indicates external customers. For a business other than R&D, marketing, sales, or the service or IT function, internal users of your services should be viewed as customers.

Note that this high-level assessment is intended to simply provide a taste for how to measure competitiveness and think quantitatively. It is not intended to be a detailed or exhaustive exercise.

Quick Self-Assessment: *Assess Competitiveness of Your Company or Business/IT Function*

RESPONSE: 0 = NOT AT ALL; 1 = LOW; 5 = HIGH

CATEGORY	QUESTION	RESPONSE
Digital IQ of Leadership	How well does your leadership understand the changes being brought about by digitalization in your industry?	_____
	How well does your leadership understand changing customer* behavior?	_____
	How clear is your leadership on the future vision for the company?	_____
	How aligned and committed is your leadership to the actions that need to be taken on the ground?	_____
	How well does the company measure progress, and how data-driven is the decision-making process in the company?	_____
LEADERSHIP Raw Score (add lines 1–5)		
Product/Service Value Propositions	How much of your product/service portfolio has been revamped in the past three years? (<10% = 1; 10–25% = 2; 25–50% = 3; 50–75% = 4; 100% = 5)	_____
	Does your company have a formal process for testing new products and services with customers* during the development cycle?	_____
	How much of your new products or services are continuously connected with customers through IoT or other telematic components? (<10% = 1; 10–25% = 2; 25–50% = 3; 50–75% = 4; 100% = 5)	_____
	How well does the company utilize data to determine improvements in products or services?	_____

Digitalization of Business Processes	What proportion of your business processes are digitalized? (<10% = 1; 10–25% = 2; 25–50% = 3; 50–75% = 4; 100% = 5)	_____
	How aligned are your business and IT on the specific objectives of digitalization (measured in outcomes or key metrics)?	_____
	How much are methods of developing digitalized processes both agile and iterative? (Do not know or <10% = 1; 10–25% = 2; 25–50% = 3; 50–75% = 4; 100% = 5)	_____
Talent Readiness	How clearly does your company communicate vision, plan, and priorities to all employees before embarking on digital initiatives?	_____
	How much does your company invest in role-based training for all employees?	_____
	How much does your company test and certify talent for its readiness once role-based training is completed?	_____
Cybersecurity	How well does your company's business leadership understand the security risks facing the organization?	_____
	How well-funded are cybersecurity initiatives in your organization?	_____

OTHER Raw Score (add lines 6-17)	

LEADERSHIP Average Score	LEADERSHIP Raw Score ÷ 12 =	

OTHER Average Score	OTHER Raw Score ÷ 12 =	

TOTAL Average Score	LEADERSHIP Average Score x OTHER Average Score =	

© Trianz 2020

Your total average score from this self-assessment will place your company/function in one of the following categories:

- Score of 0 to 1 (Pre-Digital): Your company/function has yet to grasp digitalization or undertake any serious initiatives.

- Score of 1 to 2 (Digital Beginner): Your company/function is beginning to wake up to the realities of digitalization and is just starting to undertake change.

- Score of 2 to 3 (Digital Progressive): Your company/function has understood the change that is taking place and has begun undertaking serious initiatives. Still, there is a way to go to gain management alignment or make serious, measurable progress. If you maintain the momentum, you will successfully cross the Digital Faultline, and change will be irreversible.

- Score of 3 to 4 (Digitally Advanced): Your company/function understands change. Your team is aligned, you have crossed the Digital Faultline, and you are in firm control of your strategic direction. You are adept at tracking your progress, and it is only a matter of time before you gain solid momentum.

- Score of 4 to 5 (Digitally Converged): Your company is as digital as it is currently possible to be. You are driven by data on customers, products, and services in your decision-making, initiatives, and processes. You have gained serious momentum, and it is only a matter of time before you establish a position of leadership in your role or as a company among your peers.

The scores in this simple assessment should illustrate at a high level which side of the faultline your organization is currently on. If the total score is anywhere below 2.5 on this quiz, then your organization is very much likely on the faultline or deep in crisis and you are grappling with change, still trying to make sense of it all. If you have a score of 3 or more, many of the questions here will seem basic because you are well on your way and you may be getting away from the faultline. However, you have to sustain your efforts and never look back or pause in order to evolve to a 4 or 5 score.

Digital Champions and Their Characteristics

A quick recap from the introduction—Digital Champions are the 7 percent of organizations who produce strong and consistent results from transformations. Their responses on questions related to results have been validated with other parameters in the surveys. There are a number of things that Digital Champions do differently, and their way or technique begins with experimentation and iteration and improves with each success. Everything begins with understanding, i.e., developing Digital IQ.

The first thing to note in this group is that more than two-thirds of Digital Champions rank changing customer behavior as the #1 driver of change in their industry. Ninety percent of them cite customer *behavior and* technology-fueled product innovation at the top. Competition ranks a distant third.

Generally speaking, leaders in the "average company" also understand what drives transformations, but this knowledge has not translated into a successful modernization of their businesses. Leadership teams are often not semantically aligned with a common under-

> More than two-thirds of Digital Champions rank changing customer behavior as the #1 driver of change in their industry. Ninety percent of them cite customer *behavior and* technology-fueled product innovation at the top. Competition ranks a distant third.

standing. Therefore, they are not aligned on the very purpose, priorities, or approach, or a shared sense of urgency. All this may sound simple, but it is crucial for a company to cross the Digital Faultline and grow. A glaring example of this is seen in the response to a question we asked leaders of the R&D/product management function. We asked, "How well does your CEO understand the impact of digitalization on products and services?"

More than 75 percent of respondents said their CEO either does not understand or does not fully support the investments required to transform.

When the CEO of a company does not fully understand or is unwilling to drive the change, how can management possibly be effective? Therefore, even though leaders were near unanimous on the key drivers of digitalization, very few were taking real actions. While these numbers have changed somewhat due to COVID, the fact remains that more than 90 percent of companies do not know how to transform.

However, a small percentage is making distinct choices, setting aggressive visions, and sustained efforts. Only the innovative 7 percent—Digital Champions—are transforming effectively. They understand that crossing the Digital Faultline requires reimagining products and services, as well as connecting their functions into stakeholder-experience chains. They invest in all these areas—often simultaneously. They undertake several small-to-medium initiatives as opposed to mega-initiatives. They track results and fine-tune their execution models.

The progress of Digital Champions will continue at a rapid pace and will be self-propelled to a great extent. Even though they cross the faultline and achieve a strong position on the DEEM, they do not stop. Why?

At some point, success itself becomes the game for Digital Champions. They achieve confidence and exhilaration powered by success and predictive models and know what to do. They hold a commanding lead over competition. Even though the efforts are tiring agenda, knowing their future, and professional and financial success pull them forward.

Digital Champions achieve this state after early failures, adjustments, and a relentless commitment. Though their initiatives become progressively more complex, they almost always produce targeted results. This is because their initiatives are correctly prioritized and their team uses the right methods to execute. When they fall short, they know and fix under performance. These are the characteristics of such Digital Champions:

Extreme Customer Centricity

Digital Champions constantly anticipate and provide what customers need and value. They abandon the traditional mindset or the "If we build it, they will come" or "We've been around, and we know what customers want" attitudes. The beauty of being customer-centric is that the more you engage with your customers, the more they tell you about what they want. Digital Champions home in on these continuous feedback loops and become masters of anticipation. And thus they become customer driven.

Command over Ecosystem Data

The traditional view of a company's domain is its customers, partners, suppliers, employees, and leaders. These are all connected in an organizational framework of functions, policies, and business rules. Digital Champions have a different definition of their company's ecosystem. We will study this concept of "ecosystem data" in more detail but in short, they believe that transactions, conversations, opinions, and influences *outside* their company are equally important. They harness and analyze the millions of data points generated every minute of every day. Some 75 percent of Digital Champions base their strategies almost entirely on data-driven insights.

Connected Products and Services

More than 70 percent of R&D leaders in Digital Champion companies have introduced digital interfaces and telematics, which is the process of keeping customers, devices, and services connected through the internet while gathering information about behavior, usage, and experience. The intent here is to learn from this data and generate ideas that help to improve value propositions.

Digitalized and Experience-Centric Operations

Top management alignment is a key differentiator in Digital Champions. In highly digitalized enterprises, a traditional "silo," a highly dynamic and connected transactional layer, governs customer experience and spans the enterprise. Whether the experience has to do with customers, partners, suppliers, employees, or management, all functions involved in these operations unify to deliver outstanding experiences and collect underlying data.

Digitalized Workplaces

Business processes, collaboration models, and decision-making are still manual, inefficient, and boring. Digital Champions invest in creating modern, virtual, digitalized, and global cultures and workplaces. This builds internal credibility and helps employees to better understand what digital transformation means. They align more quickly and are motivated to execute better.

Cloud-Enabled IT Infrastructures

Digital Champions use technology to power their business and empower the humans who run it. They analyze large volumes of data and deliver consistent experiences with cloud infrastructure. Besides reducing costs, the cloud dramatically accelerates the cycle time for delivering technology solutions.

Secure Business Ecosystems

The frontiers of a business are no longer limited to its walls, showrooms, and internal business processes. It is expanding into an internet-based mobile ecosystem of transactions. Along with that, access to sites, applications, documents, and data moves beyond the firewalls of the company. Digital Champions have invested heavily in ensuring that the company's data and transactions are secure. Their forethought will be a powerful advantage as cybersecurity becomes more serious and regulated.

As the adage "Rome was not built in a day" goes, Digital Champions were not born with high Digital IQ and did not develop these characteristics or achieve a leadership position overnight. They persevered through the early and rather frustrating iterations and experimented with objectives, technology, and organizational change. The latter involved increasing awareness levels, convincing, cajoling, and incentivizing employees while acting against established habits and behaviors. They persisted for years until results began to show. Once they began seeing measurable progress and understood *why* they were succeeding while competitors were failing, they left their previous methods behind. They evolved to a new set of paradigms— irreversibly—and have not stopped evolving.

Before becoming a Digital Champion, an organization first crosses the faultline when it achieves a maturity of Stage 3 (i.e.,

"Digitally Progressive"). That is when it would have developed a sufficient understanding of transformation, has demonstrated an ability to execute iteratively, and has achieved measurable success.

More importantly, it knows what needs to be done next and its movement in that direction makes change irreversible. A leader's first and foremost objective must be to reach this stage as quickly as possible.

Over time, the lead of Digital Champions grows because of the pull factor of their own success and continued investments as well as the simultaneous failure of their competitors in the industry.

The Role of Individual Leaders in Crossing the Faultline and Becoming a Digital Champion

In the TGTS data, we observed a tight correlation between a team's definition of transformation, strategy and execution models, decision-making, and the results produced. The "get it" factor, or digital IQ, becomes the single most important factor on which every other factor depends. When leaders are not self-aware or do not understand the changes in their industry, the company is in a dangerous place. A lack of a fact-based decision-making process to address these shifts further accentuates the risk. Their actions on all fronts will be incorrectly prioritized, erratic, and inefficient. The outcomes will be uncertain and will most likely be negative every single time.

On the other hand, high scores on this factor means that the collective understanding of leadership is high. This creates a compounding influence, increasing the likelihood of a team moving in the right direction. Where these leaders lack clarity, they use data and insights to realign and improve the necessary efforts. This is why the leadership score is multiplied with "other scores" and is not simply added in the previous self-assessment.

I use the word "IQ" simply because it is easy to remember. It is critical to note that no one is born with a high or low digital IQ. It is a certain perspective and a set of skills that are acquired through tenacious individual and team efforts. The whole point behind this book is that anyone can learn and acquire a high digital IQ and the accompanying leadership model in order to succeed.

Successful leaders rarely begin with a huge, complex vision or a comprehensive approach. Rather, they begin with problem or opportunity statements and follow certain fundamental approaches consistently. Over time, they get into a cycle where the results they produce give them increasing confidence. In turn, they follow these fundamentals more and more religiously and rigorously. They codify these rules to ensure that their leaders below them and extended teams do the same. Over a period of time, their entire team operates on a different set of rules compared to their competitors.

> The skills required to succeed in the Digital Age are acquired over time and constant practice. In effect, leaders in the Digital Age will not be born but made and everyone has the same opportunity.

In all, we identified ten such fundamentals, or 10 Rules, of these highly successful Digital Champions. In Part II, we use data and insights to illustrate how they use these 10 Rules to transform quickly and achieve the first goal: crossing the Digital Faultline and reclaiming a position of control.

KEY TAKEAWAYS FROM PART I: THE DIGITAL FAULTLINE

Leadership in Crisis and Upheavals—The first role of a leader is to understand the dynamics and to develop and launch a plan to get your team to safety and regain control.

6 Major Forces Create Upheavals on the Faultline:

- Changing customer behavior

- Disruptive technologies

- Unstructured innovation

- Global competition

- Many Davids and few Goliaths—the rise of start-ups

- Encroachment by the hi-tech industry

Actions: Knowledge is power. Deploy a team(s) to systematically study trends and implications of each of these six forces. Ask for regular analyses that keep you, your peers, and your teams current. Unlike general industry news and information, each of these factors and its impact are specific to your business.

Digital, Digital Transformation, and Business Transformations—Three stages of evolution. Within this, digital transformation means the reimagination of products and services and delivering high velocity experiences to all stakeholders.

Actions: Ensure a consistent understanding and definition of digital transformations within your team. If your group supports internal operations, then identify these "internal customers."

Transformations Are Rapidly Accelerating—Companies will soon find themselves staring at windows of crisis if they do not act quickly and proactively.

Actions: Irrespective of whether your current position is strong or weak, constantly develop a vision and plan for digital evolution.

Five Stages of Digital Evolution—The single biggest differentiating factor in highly successful companies, Digital Champions, is the digital IQ, or collective understanding of its leadership.

Actions: Continuously invest in digital transformation specific learning and development for your team to improve their awareness, understanding, and alignment.

A company's digital maturity is determined by the Digital IQ of its leadership; degree of digital reimagination of products and services; degree of digitalization of models and processes; and readiness of its talent and cybersecurity.

Actions: Digital IQ is an acquired asset and is developed through awareness of change and analysis of a company's internal and external data. Propagate these concepts throughout your leadership t team and begin analyzing data any which way you can.

Digital Leadership Is About Confronting Change—Understanding change and codifying a set of rules to address that change that leaders follow themselves and ensure that their teams follow too.

Actions: Share everything that you learn with your teams systematically so that the gap between you and team does not increase due to your learning. Codify your management model, train your team, and ensure follow-through.

Digital Champion Leaders make it a point to understand the new rules by which digitalization takes place and companies succeed.

Actions: Make it your business to understand the 10 Rules and the techniques to implement them in your organization.

PART II
THE 10 RULES OF HIGHLY SUCCESSFUL LEADERS IN THE DIGITAL AGE

INTRODUCTION TO THE 10 RULES OF HIGHLY SUCCESSFUL DIGITAL LEADERS

When only 7 percent in a large sample of five thousand plus leaders are highly successful in a complex endeavor, they must be doing something different *and* doing it differently. Therefore, we analyzed the TGTS data from two broad perspectives. The first was to study current status and the direction and velocity of change at an industry and functional level. These were consolidated into various industry reports on current status, visions, priorities, investments, technology platforms, implementation cycles, measures of success, and change management.

The second theme was a deeper study of the leadership of the organizations—especially the successful ones. By looking at the outcomes delivered by approximately three hundred and fifty Digital Champions, we are able to see how their leaders think, plan, and act. From this analysis emerged the 10 Rules of highly successful leaders in digital transformations. These rules are drawn from underlying patterns which are independent, uncontrollable, and continuously evolving. The first generation of successful leaders reached an understanding of these patterns initially by trial and error. Eventually, they arrived at a point after careful analysis where they accepted the supremacy of these patterns, much like the laws of physics. Rather than challenging them or ignoring them because they are daunting, they think about the "so what." In other words, if this is the pattern, what do I do about it, how do I respond or take advantage?

Each of these 10 Rules is described in an individual chapter and in a particular sequence, as one rule builds on the other. Although presented one at a time, the 10 Rules must NOT be viewed as independent but as a holistic set wherein one Rule influences others. Therefore, leaders will not achieve much by following a few favorites while ignoring the others. The sequence is laid out in the table here:

THE 10 RULES OF LEADING AND SUCCEEDING IN THE DIGITAL AGE	
Rule #1:	Prioritize Customer Centricity over Competitive Differentiation
Rule #2:	Replace Assumptions with Data Analysis
Rule #3:	Disrupt Yourself before the Hi-Tech Industry Does It for You
Rule #4:	Insist on Technology-Enabled Value Propositions
Rule #5:	Break Functional Silos to Become an Experience-Driven Organization
Rule #6:	Learn How to Use Digital Technologies to Be an Effective Business Leader
Rule #7:	Strategize and Execute in Quick Iterations
Rule #8:	Technology Does Not Make Transformations Effective—People Do! Invest in Your Talent
Rule #9:	Measure Progress with Data and KPIs. Be Relentless—Even after Crossing the Digital Faultline.
Rule #10:	Be Aggressive but Set Realistic Stakeholder Expectations

Each chapter in which a rule is described begins with an overview followed by elaboration on why and how. The idea is simply to enable an understanding of what Digital Champions do. To illustrate key points, I have used certain frameworks abstracted from underlying data. I have also provided simple analytics of the results produced by Digital Champions to illustrate the power of these rules. In the case of a few select rules, I have highlighted certain concepts and techniques in more detail—going beyond the data.

COVID-19 has clearly played a role in accelerating the disruption due to digitalization. While a lot of this is discussed within the chapter, I have also provided a summary of the COVID effect at the end of a chapter wherever applicable.

As a final thought before we get started, I do not go into the persona of leaders themselves. Similarly, I have not covered how these 10 Rules are implemented and how a reader can adopt them. The idea is to keep the discussion focused on the 10 Rules themselves and how they affect successful digital transformation.

Once we understand the 10 Rules, we will study the persona of highly successful leaders, their technique, tireless commitment, and discipline in applying these 10 Rules. Finally, we will utilize a playbook to adopt, customize, and use the 10 Rules to drive your own digital transformation.

So let us advance from understanding the forces on the Digital Faultline and evolution of companies to the 10 Rules that Digital Champion leaders employ to tame these forces and control their destinies.

PRIORITIZE CUSTOMER CENTRICITY OVER COMPETITIVE DIFFERENTIATION

Let me begin this discussion about customers by sharing a thousand-year-old Indian parable about six wise blind men and an elephant.

Legend has it that one day an elephant was brought to a nearby town. Elders from the town invited these revered wise men to help them understand the strange animal they were encountering for the first time. And so the wise men traveled all the way from their hermitage in the forests to the town square where it was on display. With some help, each of them stood at a different part of the elephant to feel its body.

The first blind man placed his hand on the animal's trunk and said, "An elephant is very similar to a large, thick snake." The second man felt its ear and said, "It is an animal but with the qualities of a bird, for it has wings." The third wise man felt the side of the elephant and described it as a wall. The fourth felt its tail and claimed that the elephant was like rope. The fifth blind man felt the leg of the elephant and said an elephant is "like a pillar in a temple." The spectators watched in amusement but quietly so because the five wise men were otherwise well-respected.

The sixth wise man quietly listened to what everyone said. He then asked a few spectators to measure the animal's length and height, combined their views, and described what an elephant really was.

The message in the parable is about the illusion of "knowing" but not knowing fully or correctly. It also shows how our prior experience or knowledge can mislead us into wrong conclusions. While the first five blind men correctly described what they touched and felt, their descriptions of an elephant were inaccurate. They were also based on their understanding of similar animals. The sixth wise man, by piecing the information together, more accurately figured out that it was an extremely large four-legged animal with a long trunk, a big head, and two large ears.

We can compare customers in the Digital Age to the big elephant. We may think we know them because we have been doing business with them for a long time. However, given the change they are going through, our experience-based view is merely telling us what the customers used to be. It does not tell us who they are today, and much less who they will become in terms of their needs, preferences, and behaviors. As in the case of the blind men, there are many aspects to this elephant that must be explored for a full understanding. Only by examining behavioral data, product-service needs, alternative value propositions, and their changing economic situations will we be able to know where the customers are today or predict how they will evolve.

New Influences on Customer Life Cycle

As discussed earlier, consumer behavior is being heavily influenced by ever-increasing choices of personal computers, mobile phones, gaming devices, and digital content. The full impact of this is more directly visible in B2C industries, though, indirectly, it is equally strong in B2B.

Figure 7 describes the entire relationship cycle between customers and a company and the role of digitalization in the process. The influence of digital begins with how customers first consider a product or service or their "purchase triggers." It continues with comparisons of value, online buying, consumption, and eventual replacement of a product or service.

FIGURE 7. DIGITAL CUSTOMER RELATIONSHIP CYCLE

PURCHASE TRIGGERS

- Need / utility
- Technology & convenience
- Games & online content
- Friends & social pressure
- Social media & influencers

CUSTOMERS **VALUE...**

- ROTI (i.e., their time)
- Fit with digital habits
- Utility over brand
- Coolness factor
- Causes (the environment, health, etc.)

CUSTOMERS **EXPECT...**

- Digital interfaces
- Digital content
- Sharing
- Proactive service & support

CUSTOMERS **BUY** ACCORDING TO...

- Income availability
- Spending priorities
- Price sensitivity
- Comparative shopping
- Utility vs. brand
- Digital commerce

CUSTOMER DIVERSIFIERS

Gender   Age   Ethnicity

© Trianz Research (Trasers) 2021

In each stage, customers research online before they buy or engage digitally. This is even more true since COVID, and we do not meet customers in retail stores or conference rooms as we used to. This dramatic reduction in physical interactions has resulted in us not being able to see or feel customer reactions and emotions. That is where the similarity with the elephant and the blind men parable begins.

Age, ethnicity, gender, education, region, and consumer or business segment biases make understanding customer behavior and digital influences even more difficult. For example, most millennials in the US today earn less than their parents did at their age, whereas it is the opposite in India or China. Rightfully so, millennials are budget- and savings-conscious; they care about health and the environment, they value opinions in their networks, and they treat digital as essential.

Therefore, millennials may not even value a product or service that has been a routine need for prior generations. This generational shift in needs and priorities is why products and services such as cars, houses, jewelry, life insurance, or cable TV are not on the shopping list for millennials.

This is not a marketing problem. Rather, it is a massive shift in the value that these emerging customers ascribe to products and services of any type, given various income and social changes they are experiencing.

In addition, COVID-19 has broken the continuity of various tracking and analyses of consumer behavior. We now do not know how deep or permanent COVID-triggered changes will be.

On the other hand, buying decisions in B2B markets are group decisions that make customer behavior much more difficult to understand. A uniqueness of their company, changing needs, or definitions of value drive business customers to often seek a tailoring of products and services. Regardless of the segment, products and services must be continually tested and refined until "customer need vs. value" sweet spots are found.

Figure 8 shows the competitiveness of product/service portfolios of over five hundred companies as analyzed in the TGTS data. The analysis compares investments made by companies to modernize their portfolio vs. a digitalization of their product introduction process. The primary conclusions are outlined next.

FIGURE 8. PORTFOLIO COMPETITIVENESS MATRIX

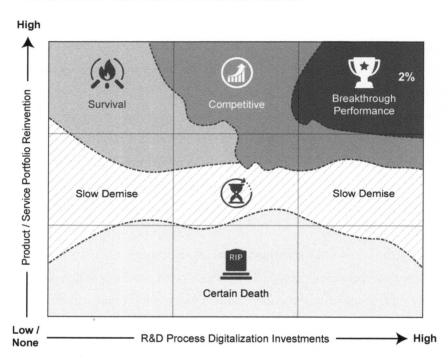

© Trianz Research (Trasers) 2021

A company will not succeed unless customers see value in the product and are impressed by the entire experience. Highly successful companies achieve superior performance by continuously improving the appeal of their products and services (y-axis) and then accelerating development cycles (x-axis).

Conversely, 30 percent or more of companies, i.e., ones in the lower squares, will simply fade away or perish because customers no longer consider their products or services to be useful.

Successful companies therefore extensively use a "sixth wise man," or data, to understand customers and their definition of value. They methodically analyze the vast amount of customer data in their business ecosystems to understand changing needs and behaviors and make necessary adjustments. To understand why customer centricity trumps competition, let us first look how Digital Champions define "customers."

Customers Are External *and* Internal

When speaking of customers, by default we think of external customers who buy a company's products. In the late 1980s and 1990s, however, management theories such as "total quality," "BPR," and "ISO" popularized the idea that every function is a customer to another. This theme of internal customers becomes even more important in digital transformations.

The basic concept in this philosophy is that every business function in a company has customers—it is just that they are either external or internal. For example, marketing and sales are "customers" of finance. R&D/product management is the "customer" of manufacturing. Manufacturing and service are "customers" of supply chain, and so on.

This concept also considers those employees, partners, and suppliers who work on behalf of the company as customers. As we see throughout this book, treating these audiences in the same way as you treat external customers has a great impact on transformations.

Adjacent Functions as Internal Customers

As companies launch new products and services, they begin to set new expectations of value and highly digitalized experiences. For example, companies that are successful online do not create only a digital sales process but also build the required digital commerce capabilities, catalogs, and pricing models. These, however, are the responsibilities of marketing and finance. Similarly, great order fulfillment and delivery experiences are essential, but these are responsibilities of the supply chain function.

The internally disconnected organization that hands off the customer from one department to another will not succeed in today's environment. Successful leaders, therefore, view their peer functions as internal customers. They listen to these internal customers and deliver the digitalization capabilities or integrations they need as required.

Given that external customers want simple and minimal interactions, a company must now view itself as a chain-link that delivers a unified experience to the external customer. When any one function lags or is disconnected, the entire customer experience breaks down.

External Partners and Suppliers

In an environment of changing relationships, successful companies build a network of committed relationships. By giving partners and suppliers the same importance as end customers, successful companies show a higher level of commitment. By integrating them digitally wherever needed, they create unified customer experiences in their ecosystems. In turn, partners reciprocate by becoming advocates of the brand and sharing critical market feedback. Ideas from such feedback go into improving products, services, and experiences.

Employees of the Company

Successful companies see employees as their most critical assets, but they first enable them for high performance. Today, employees face a contradiction between their experiences as buyers of various products and their experiences while working. For example, an employee working in sales may shop online in their personal lives by default but is forced to take orders on the phone while working for their company because it does not sell online. What does this contrasting experience say about the company to the employee? Nothing good.

Employees are also affected by the COVID pandemic, which has confined them to their homes and forced them to switch between work and taking care of their families. While COVID may be brought under control, remote working is very much here to stay. Successful companies treat employees just as they treat customers, which eventually results in higher productivity, collaboration, and lower stress levels.

The first impact of a digitalizing processes is that it makes work easier. Internal testing by employees also provides critical insights into customer behavior and their likely response to new value propositions. Digital initiatives are, therefore, better understood and more effective when the dichotomy of employee experience is narrowed or eliminated.

Why Customers Are More
Important than Competitors

TGTS research shows that most companies do not truly understand the basic definition of digital transformation. As we have discussed in this book, *digital transformation is the reimagination of products and services from a customer point of view, and the reinvention of business value chains into customer and stakeholder-experience chains.*

Notice that there is no mention of "competitor" in our definition.

The problem begins with a lack of a holistic understanding of customers. Data show that over 70 percent of companies have not invested in the underlying data infrastructure necessary to analyze changing customer segmentation, needs, budget allocations, preferences, and buying process. Many default to monitoring the competition and working hard on either imitating or differentiating. Even among the ones that do understand the importance of customers, very few have successfully adapted to these changes.

The consequence of being competitor-focused as opposed to being customer-focused is that we are simply adding several more blind men to describe the elephant.

Let us take the case of three companies: A, B, and C. Let us say Company A is launching a new product for customers in their industry. However, A's product definition and marketing strategy is constantly influenced by its larger competitors, B and C. Here is why this strategy is flawed. Given what we know, it very likely that B and C's understanding of customers is likely incomplete or backward-looking. Much like the blind men in the parable, the description of customers by competitors is unreliable at best and damaging at worst—unless the competitors have transformed successfully as evidenced by data. Therefore, a preoccupation with B and C will only lead Company A to make poor decisions on product features, pricing, branding, sales strategies, and customer engagement models.

> Much like the blind men in the parable, the description of customers by competitors is unreliable at best and damaging at worst—unless the competitors have transformed successfully as evidenced by data.

Take, for example, the US retail industry from ten years ago. While Sears, Kmart, JC Penney,

Macy's, and Walmart were preoccupied with each other, they did not see or accept that customers were rapidly moving to online shopping. By the time they understood the new customer buying behaviors and Amazon's digital model, it was too late. Amazon's lead in understanding its customers, digital commerce capabilities, global scale of economy, low-price guarantee, and high quality soon became insurmountable. The only companies to successfully respond on a comparable scale are Walmart, Target, and niche players such as Best Buy, Wayfair, etc. Ask anyone what is important in retail today and their answer will be customer data.

How Customer Centricity Influences Competitive Positions

I do not mean that one should totally ignore competitors, their products, their services, or their competitive strategies. Leaders must certainly keep an eye on them but only if they are better and more successful. However, continuously understanding one's own customers, launching new products, services, experiences, and tracking sales, satisfaction, and brand loyalty data are essential. Once a team gets into a groove of success, the challenge shifts to keeping the lead, differentiation, and velocity. That is when competitors become important.

Industry structures will therefore keep shifting on the faultline. The forces that affect a company's competitive position will be quite different, and a

> I do not mean that one should totally ignore competitors, their products, their services, or their competitive strategies. Leaders must certainly keep an eye on them but only if they are better and more successful.

strong customer focus will be the main theme around which new industry structures will revolve (Figure 9).

FIGURE 9. CUSTOMER-DRIVEN GROWTH FRAMEWORK

© Trianz Research (Trasers) 2021

Being customer driven means always being ahead of the customer. Besides keeping an eye on their key competitors, Digital Champions master four disciplines to gain validation, generate momentum, growth, and strong market influence:

> Being customer driven means always being ahead of the customer.

- **Understanding Customer Behavior**: A data-driven understanding of decision-makers, their evaluation and buying process, and how they engage with the company.

- **Understanding Disruptive Technologies:** While technology in general is a vast subject, from a customer's point of view, only two clusters are relevant. The first is the "products and services technology" cluster. This is technology that is used in an industry for designing, manufacturing, distributing, delivering products, or providing customer support. The second cluster is "customer technology," i.e., technologies that play a role in the customers' digital hangouts, tools, and buying process and the in-relationship life cycle.

- **New Value Propositions and Connected Experiences:** Developing, testing, and launching corresponding value propositions and underlying experiences.

- **Velocity of Digital Innovation:** A redesigned process that incorporates customer feedback with a built-in flexibility for adjustments and helps deliver new products at as high a velocity as possible.

By mastering these four interrelated disciplines and monitoring the influence, success, or failure of competitors, Digital Champions better predict customer behavior. They use digital technology within the context of their product or service better. They continuously deliver superior value and experiences at a higher velocity. The confluence of their success in these disciplines helps in always staying ahead of customers and more market influence. This further translates into better supplier, distribution, retail, and service provider relationships, as well as superior pricing and margins.

While all this sounds straightforward in the external customer context, not every leader in an organization understands customers if the focus of their role is internal. For example, HR is focused on employees, procurement is focused on suppliers, information technology is providing technology services, and so on. But without understanding the concept of customers, it is hard to deliver connected experiences.

Successful companies ensure that their entire top management has a shared understanding of external customers. They align their leadership around the vision, relevant technologies, products, services, innovation, and drivers of customer satisfaction. This top management alignment enables superior execution, results, and sustained competitive advantage.

When companies start succeeding, a symbiotic relationship begins to form with customers. Customers do not want to let go of this new, hard-found value proposition or an experience they love. When they are convinced that the company understands and sincerely cares about them, they trust, rely, and even depend on the relationship.

In effect, the more a company succeeds, the more its customers are vested in its success, which creates what can be called "reinforcing feedback." In such a mutually beneficial engagement, customers will provide even more feedback and data. This, in turn, puts the team on the path to continued innovation, growth, and better relationships. We do not have to look too far for evidence of success in this customer-driven growth framework. Companies such as Amazon Web Services and Microsoft Azure in the cloud, Apple and Samsung in the cell phone business, and Google in the search space are clear examples.

They all know their customers very well; customers tell them what they want and where they are going, and the companies respond by improving themselves. The only circumstances in which a competitor will be a valuable source of ideas is when they are technologically ahead, if their products and services are doing better, and their digital growth is faster.

The COVID Effect on Rule #1

COVID-19 has affected customers in every industry in every country around the world. Besides physical health and loss of lives, the effects are social and economic.

Socially speaking, people's lives, routines, and relationships have been seriously disrupted. While social structures are intact and have played a positive role, human behavior will change to a great degree. Sociologists believe that there will be two extremes. A small minority may become highly introverted and cautious, while others may become outgoing and bold. However, most of the general population is likely to become more cautious, maintaining social distancing and limiting physical activities. Such behavior is likely to continue for a long time.

From an economic perspective, worldwide GDP is likely to reduce by 5 percent or more. In the United States alone, an estimated twenty-seven to thirty million—or about 20 percent of the workforce—lost employment. In other parts of the world, the effects are less severe due to lower costs of living and help from extended families. Consumer behavior has turned conservative, and spending on discretionary items will remain depressed. Cheaper online alternatives, such as learning, health and exercise, reading, entertainment, communication, and gaming, will become more popular.

The Key Takeaway: though understanding customer behavior was difficult before COVID-19, expect it to become harder. It is now even more critical to focus on understanding COVID's effect on existing customers' behaviors, budgets, preferences, and definitions of value in your business category. As discussed in this chapter, making your product/service value propositions compelling and rapidly validating with customers is even more fundamental.

Most of your competitors may still not understand customers; many may not even survive or may no longer be relevant. Customers will be even more important than competitors.

RULE #2

REPLACE ASSUMPTIONS WITH DATA ANALYSIS

Why Traditional Assumptions Fail on the Faultline

In his classic seventeenth-century treatise *On War*, Prussian General Karl von Clausewitz says, "Everything is simple in war but simple does not mean easy." This is because of a certain friction that emerges when two sides confront each other in battle. In this contest of strategies, weaponry, bravery, will, and leadership, the assumptions made by one side clash with those of the other side. When these assumptions go wrong, friction results.

Business in any industry today is akin to a battlefield, just a different kind. The objectives are to gain market share, revenue, and profits; to grow; and ultimately, to create brand positioning and loyalty. Much as in the development of a battlefield strategy, business leaders also make assumptions or engage consultants to help fill the gaps. What makes it even more complex is that the business battlefield has many players and not just two opposing sides. But as we have seen, conditions on this battlefield are highly dynamic, and windows of opportunity are shrinking for all players.

The use of assumptions, prior experiences, or collecting data only when needed is an approach that will always fall short. When change is taking place at a massive scale, such perspectives will be outdated and never holistic. By the time data is collected, the landscape has shifted, making obsolete any strategies developed from the data.

For strategy to be truly effective in the Digital Age, it must be highly adaptive to change. And to be inherently adaptive, it must rely on continuously collected and predictive insights.

Data: The Open Secret in Your Ecosystem

The traditional definition of a business limits it to its customers, suppliers, and employees interacting with each other in during commercial transactions. While it is true that a large part of business is transacted between these audiences, a new and broader definition has taken shape. In this concept, each business is an ecosystem that extends into competitors, partners, regulators, and influencers. Before digital techniques came into existence, companies relied on manual processes and had little or no integration with these stakeholders in their ecosystem. With their irregular engagement, companies didn't take them seriously other than to review them periodically.

Digital platforms, such as websites, portals, mobile apps, real-time interfaces, IoT devices, and social media, now connect players on a perpetual basis. This alters the nature and frequency of the engagement between various stakeholders in a company's ecosystem. Their interactions may be nontransactional but are continuous in the form of conversations about new patterns, research, technology, innovations, or opinions that influence others. Data is now being created continuously, and it provides important clues into the regular business, new trends, and what players in the industry could be up to.

When a company analyzes all this data regularly, it develops a holistic idea of its stakeholders, has friendly, competitive, or game-changing dynamics, and makes fact-based decisions. It also begins to anticipate what customers want or how to quietly tackle their issues without having to disturb the customer. One reason why customers do not receive letters from Facebook or Instagram is because they are regularly connected with their customers. Therefore, there is no need to send letters. Technologies such as artificial intelligence take rule-based and automatic actions to a whole other level.

That the boundaries of a business extend to non-transactional stakeholders and data gets generated every second are two very important aspects that every company and leader must be aware of. There are three levels of data being created in any ecosystem, twenty-four hours a day and 365 days a year. Let us review these a bit more holistically (Figure 10).

FIGURE 10. ECOSYSTEM DATA

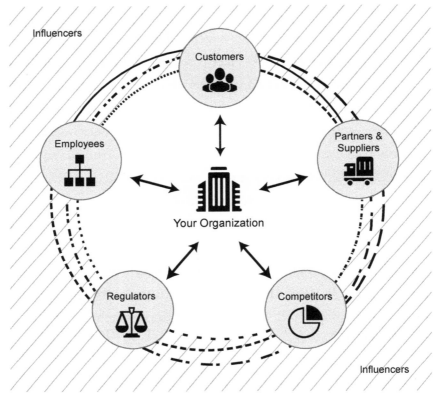

© Trianz Research (Trasers) 2021

Enterprise Transactional Data

This first-level data is created by transactions within a company or with external stakeholders. This type of bidirectional and transactional data is well known and foundational to all companies. Examples include sales quotes, sales orders, shipment information, purchase orders, new employee onboarding, technical support issues, etc. In technology-invested companies, such data on customer, supplier, and employee transactions is stored within the company's IT systems such as CRM, ERP, HRMS, etc.

Stakeholder Transactional Data

This second-level data is created due through engagement between stakeholders, often without the company's involvement. Examples might be a regulator pursuing a competitor for a certain action, a supplier signing a major contract with one of its biggest competitors, a top-level industry executive joining another company, or a tech company that provides technology to the industry announcing a new breakthrough, and so on.

Such data is often found in the form of announcements in the media, regulatory filings, "pay for use" databases, news articles, and press releases. While they may not involve the company directly, it is immensely affected by the transactions behind the data. It is important to track this data and become predictive, as its patterns are often indicators of an industry trend or a major event.

Influencer Network Data

The third and most complicated type of data in the ecosystem are opinions expressed on various business platforms, in forums, and on social media. In today's empowered internet environment, various audiences talk about the company, a product/service, competitor, technology, or a trend all the time. Networks of influence target specific stakeholder groups or followers. This "influencer network data" is sometimes invisible to leadership since most companies outside of the tech industry do not naturally connect with these networks. However, gaining an understanding and building an effective influencer network is absolutely critical to ultimately influencing customers.

Two more points about data itself. All data is not naturally quantitative in the beginning. In fact, most data in an ecosystem are unstructured and reside outside of the four walls of the company. Examples of unstructured data are a video interview given by a customer, an email complaint written by a partner, or a chat on Twitter about the company.

Using technology, each type of this unstructured, or "big data," as it is called, can be converted into quantitative terms. As an example, the likes of Netflix, Facebook, Instagram, YouTube, and others have mastered the analysis of this big data. They know what each type of audience thinks, talks about, does, or even wants before the audience says so. Given that content consumption is the business of these companies, this analysis then feeds the right content and ads for that user group without any intervention.

Every company has customers, prospects, and influencers with whom it may or may not yet have transactions. Successful companies understand who these potentials are, what they seek, and what they express—and proactively improve products/services and position them correctly for those potentials. Knowledge gained from all the three layers of data help companies to anticipate needs, drive strategies, and convert prospects into customers.

Secondly, it is important to note that these ecosystems are not restricted to customer-facing groups such as sales, marketing, or customer service. Rather, they exist for every function across the enterprise. For example, in the case of R&D or product innovation, the ecosystem would be comprised of customers, competitors, technology providers, suppliers, design partners, regulators, and marketing. Similarly, the human capital ecosystem would be employees, management, prospective talent, service providers, thought leaders, influencers, regulators, change management experts, competitors, etc.

Successful leaders develop a deep awareness of their ecosystem, invest in appropriate data foundations, unify that data, and analyze it continuously. Besides knowing their stakeholders, they understand their own digital readiness, their main competitors, and gaps and adjust their vision and priorities as necessary.

Data-Driven Insights Break Silos and Accelerate Decision-Making

In the absence of a shared definition of digital transformation, most leaders will develop vision, strategy, or priorities that are not aligned with what really matters to customers. This is where the disconnect begins between the definition of digital transformation from a customer perspective and management action.

In the background is the rising pressure from corporate boards and CEOs to adapt quickly. Leaders say they know they must transform and must do so quickly, but they struggle with how to do it. How does one develop a customer-centric vision, strategy, and priorities while dealing with the day-to-day realities on the Digital Faultline?

The answer again is in data. The more an enterprise understands, analyzes, and interprets the data being generated within the company and its environment, the more it begins to replace assumptions with facts. The more data-driven insights are shared and discussed, the more management viewpoints begin to converge. Everyone quickly realizes that stakeholder expectations reflected by data are more important than their personal differences and biases. This convergence first leads to a common definition of digital

> The more an enterprise understands, analyzes, and interprets the data being generated within the company and its environment, the more it begins to replace assumptions with facts.

transformation as it applies to their company. Then follows faster and more objective decision-making around strategic priorities.

While this sounds logical, the process of arriving at such a consensus is not easy. Long-established habits, organizational dynamics, and turf battles can often override the practical logic that emerges from data-driven insights. Companies that do not develop their game plan quickly using data will miss a window of opportunity that has shrunk dramatically since COVID. There is no time for internal games and questioning what data says. Companies must get their strategy and execution right the first time.

While most companies struggle with these internal challenges, Digital Champions are breaking away at an accelerating pace with strong leadership and timely data-driven decision-making. Highly successful companies use data and analytics in all their major decisions (Figure 11).

FIGURE 11. HOW DIGITAL CHAMPIONS USE DATA IN DECISION-MAKING

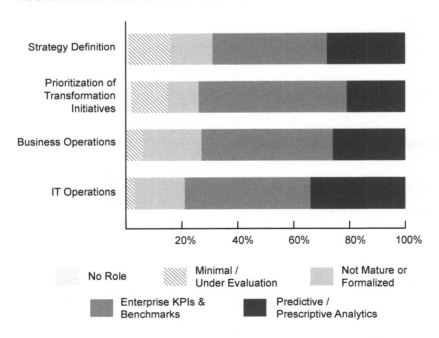

Data and Analytics Sophistication Levels

Organizations typically go through four stages of maturity in building the necessary technology capabilities and use of data and analytics. These are as follows:

- **Stage 1–Reporting:** The first stage is the ability to generate reports across the business; they will all know what happened yesterday. While capability lies in the business applications companies use on an everyday basis, it is critical to configure it appropriately.

- **Stage 2–Business Intelligence:** The second stage of maturity is business intelligence and dashboards, or the ability to know what is happening today.

- **Stage 3–Predictive Analytics:** By investing in data science-based algorithms, companies develop an ability to predict what is likely to happen in their business. This is described as using predictive analytics.

- **Stage 4–Prescriptive Analytics and AI:** Once an organization gains command over data and understands human behaviors, it can generate prescriptive insights. In many cases, these are further automated using AI technology, which guides business processes to outcomes without human intervention. AI ultimately reduces costs and accelerates business process.

Most companies today still have only basic reporting capabilities. TGTS data also shows that more than 70 percent of companies do not yet understand what measures or KPIs to use in the digital context. Contrasted, Digital Champion companies have invested in data and analytics for years and have gone through various stages of maturity. Newcomers to the game have to make sustained investments and find ways to catch up or leapfrog. Ultimately, such digital enterprises will accumulate powerful data and predictive capabilities that accelerate their growth. They will disrupt legacy players who are not data-driven, make the wrong choices, and cannot keep pace.

However, companies lagging behind do not have the luxury of time nor do they have many opportunities to develop the right strategy to catch up. The only way to catch up on lost time is by leapfrogging to predictive analytics as soon as possible, regardless of the current state of their analytics maturity. The key here is to race to those insights which will reveal the right customer and competitive priorities, the gaps, and the actions necessary to gain relevance and forward momentum.

> Digital Champion companies have invested in data and analytics for years and have gone through various stages of maturity. Newcomers to the game have to make sustained investments and find ways to catch up or leapfrog.

The COVID Effect on Rule #2

COVID-19 has impacted business models in most industries. The common themes are digital customer interactions from sales to service and remote working across all major functions within a company. There are also major shifts and new consumption patterns signaled by the arrival of entirely new product and service categories that promote better lifestyles, health, and well-being. Many of these are being launched by nascent companies, indicating that start-ups that were born digital are now finding a sustained appeal.

The Key Takeaway: the role of data and analytics in the beginning of the COVID cycle was to simply to help make sense of volatility in revenues, demand, and adjusting various dimensions of supply. The idea was to make quick adjustments to minimize financial losses, maintain engagement with the customer base, and transition employees to remote working.

The role of data now is entirely different. It is to study and predict customer behavior and the degree of shift or permanency of new preferences, wallet sizes, and buying and consumption patterns. It is to find opportunities to accelerate and drive efficiency throughout the value chain. Companies that were well invested into data and analytics will find the marginal investments to be easy—their competitive lead will only increase. Companies that did not make adequate investments must rapidly reprioritize their budgets and management focus to build predictive capabilities.

After all, one cannot solve a problem or grasp an opportunity without understanding where it is today or where it is going tomorrow.

RULE #3

DISRUPT YOURSELF BEFORE HI-TECH DOES IT FOR YOU

Over the past decade, the hi-tech industry has steadily and success-fully encroached upon other industries. There are many examples to illustrate this. Tesla has turned the entire automotive industry upside down. Uber and Lyft have reinvented the taxi business. PayPal, Stripe, and Square compete with Visa and Mastercard in payment process-ing. Electronic Arts pioneered a whole new gaming industry and Microsoft changed the way games are played. Netflix, Apple, and Google changed the entire media and entertainment model, forcing Disney to reinvent. Airbnb has changed hospitality. Amazon is now in the grocery business, thanks to its acquisition of Whole Foods. DoorDash has created a new way to order food.

Except for Microsoft and Amazon, each of these tech companies started in the Silicon Valley. They grew from a concept to a well-funded organization that delivered great products. These cool products were quickly adopted by local audiences, and eventually they became global giants. These companies also command the highest profit margins in the industries they have encroached on. As an example, Apple today has less than 15 percent of the global smartphone market share but takes about 33 percent of revenue and more than 65 percent of the entire industry's profits.

Traditional and established companies in every industry are finding it hard to counter hi-tech's drive. They are unable to combat the financial strength that comes from premium revenue, profit, and cash flow. Hi-tech companies grow and retain customers, sell at great margins, generate hordes of cash, and invest in new businesses—all at a blistering pace. Some, such as Tesla and Uber, go to an extreme—often taking huge sustained losses while launching completely new businesses. What do asteroid mining or satellite communications have to do with Tesla's automotive business? Nothing. Similarly, there is no relationship between groceries, entertainment, and online retail, as in the case of Amazon. Tesla and Amazon just feel like being in those businesses because they see opportunities to reinvent those industries.

The question established companies in all industries must ask is "What strategies are we going to use to counterattack?" The answer lies in first understanding hi-tech's sources of inspiration and their cycle of reinvention. These factors combine to provide a deadly competitive advantage that is not going away anytime soon. The good news for legacy companies that by embracing technology disrupting themselves, they can turn hi-tech's game against it. Because if they don't disrupt themselves, it's only a matter of time before hi-tech does it.

Hi-Tech Is Powered by Data Analytics

The hi-tech industry sells products and services to every other industry around the world—but the game only begins with the sale. From digitalized applications, smart agents in their software, and

IoT in physical products, hi-tech has access to business data. From search, social media, gaming, online retail, or online entertainment, they have access to consumer data. If you are watching a movie on Amazon Prime and have Alexa at home, Amazon knows where you are and how you connect, multitask, and what your choices are. The same applies if you are listening to music on a smartphone or searching for something on Google. By analyzing usage and social data in their business, hi-tech has developed an understanding of user behaviors and needs. In addition, they create data-sharing partnerships among themselves. This gives them access to data tracked by others to maintain immediacy to market while acknowledging each other's positions.

The misuse of consumer data by some players in the form of reselling it for ad sales, adjunct sales, politics, or downright manipulation is undeniable, and there is no excuse for it. The downright primitive controls on privacy and content in social media platforms cannot and should not be tolerated by governments anywhere. However, the argument of the non-social-media tech is that it has largely used these data insights for conceptualizing, designing, and launching new products, services, and making things better for consumers and business customers.

Netflix provides an excellent example of usage of data and analytics:

Twenty years ago, Netflix operated from a warehouse in Los Gatos, Silicon Valley. Their original business was shipping entertainment DVDs to their members, who would get five DVDs per month for a fixed fee. Customers would register, pay Netflix (in advance), order DVDs from a catalog on the Netflix website, and mail them back after viewing. Along the way came ideas for creating a new digital entertainment value proposition. Netflix brought the theater to homes by perfecting streaming content—and in the process changed how digital content is distributed and consumed.

The centerpiece of the Netflix strategy is customer data. From the moment that customers login, Netflix tracks their data. By analyzing ethnicity, gender, age, and language, they can segment their customers. By monitoring searches, preferences, and attention spans, they can suggest content. They are always evolving and expanding their online library, providing each customer segment what it wants to see. They can see customer issues, complaints, and tech support questions in real time, often even before a customer complains. And even after having become a diverse and reliable entertainment sources, they keep reinventing.

Except for Disney, which launched its own streaming service, the rest of the entertainment industry became a farm of content producers. Netflix probably does not share customer preference and consumption intelligence with content producers. It may just be buying content, which it resells while keeping a good chunk of revenue and profit.

Using data for continuous adaptation, Netflix changed an industry that had been dominated by Hollywood for a more than a century. In 2020, Netflix was one of the most awarded studios, taking the crown from the legendary studios of Hollywood. It has built every major component of its business organically and did not make a single studio acquisition. This was perhaps because Netflix leaders did not believe an acquisition would align with their strategy or culture, much less enhance it. Netflix is now a $10 billion entertainment industry giant—and that is just one example of encroachment by tech.

The Cycle of Value Proposition Reinvention

In studying example after example of digital disruption, a pattern emerges across both B2B and B2C industries. At its heart is an iterative cycle of innovation based on a consolidation and analysis of customer, product, and technology data (Figure 12). From this data emerges a "reimagination" that refines or aggregates an existing proposition or delivers a completely new one.

FIGURE 12. THE CYCLE OF PRODUCT/SERVICE DISRUPTION

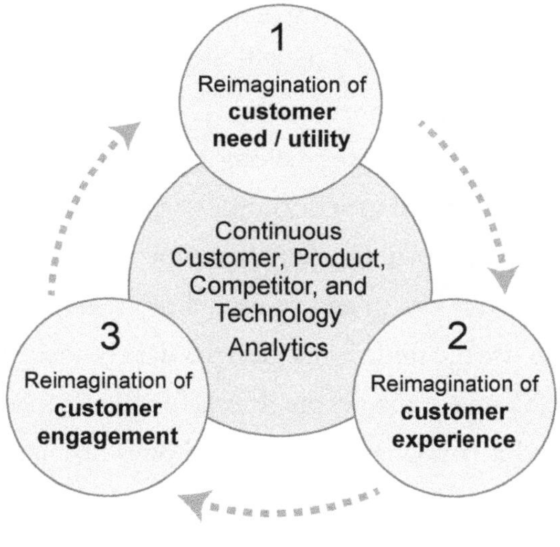

© Trianz Research (Trasers) 2021

It is this cycle of reinvention that aggregated voice, video, text messaging, camera, and even the PC and unlimited apps into the smartphone. This transformation of the phone into a personal digital platform came from the tech industry. AT&T, Lucent, Bell Labs, Siemens, NTT, and Ericsson—all major players that once shaped telephony for the whole world—were not the innovators. It was Motorola that invented the first handheld, called the DynaTac, and later condensed it into a palm-sized phone called StarTac in 1996. This was improved upon by Nokia, which shrunk it, added text as a feature, and then ruled the industry for the next two decades.

Another example of reimagining value propositions can be seen in electric cars. Tesla, a Silicon Valley start-up, introduced the electric car even as the entire industry was dismissive about the idea. In the span of a decade, and despite numerous struggles, Tesla has emerged as the global leader in electric cars. Even as it disrupts the passenger car segment, Tesla has set its sights on autonomous, electric, and full-sized cargo trucks. Tesla has also encroached on the aeronautics, space, solar, and battery industries with SpaceX and Tesla Solar. With the recent acquisition of Maxwell, Tesla will become a maker of batteries for consumer electronics.

Finally, we have an example of making a value proposition obsolete in the genetics arena. Several genetics companies are using DNA technologies and a mapping of the human genome with a dual purpose. They provide DNA test kits to people to identify their ancestral information. They also use the underlying genetics data to identify and help prevent diseases. These companies are thus helping researchers to create new treatments while making a range of old ones obsolete. Some are going even further. By identifying defective genes in human embryos, they can alert parents and help to prevent defective births.

The centerpiece of these cycles is the continuous collection and analysis of customer, product, and technology data. This gives birth to new concepts of value (Phase 1 in Figure 12). This value is then packaged and delivered to customers through innovative and engaging experiences (Phase 2). As customers use the new products or services, the company collects their data from digital and continuous engagement. As the data comes in, the hi-tech disruptor no longer needs to make assumptions or track legacy industry players.

Their data analysis fuels cycle after cycle of value and experience refinement (Phase 3).

The hi-tech industry is successful at introducing new products and services because it has combined all the pieces necessary to create a cohesive, well-financed innovation framework that spins out products and services continuously.

It is called "digital disruption" because the entire process of acquiring customers, delivering value, collecting and analyzing data, and refining the value proposition is largely done digitally.

The fast pace is a Silicon Valley culture set by a desire to race each other—and it is a pace that the rest of world cannot yet understand or keep up with. It is accentuated further by the company-wide adoption of cloud.

Entrenched companies in various industries are falling prey to hi-tech because they have not invested in data analysis and they do not fully understand this concept of digital disruption. Compounding the problem is a culture of resistance to making changes to legacy cash-cow products or services. This plays perfectly to the strategy of hi-tech because revenue or profit is not its initial goal. The goal is to prove the concept and acquire a critical mass of customers. The death of iconic brands in recent times was not due to an inability of individuals to grasp these concepts. It was death by a broader culture of resistance and defending old turf.

Secret Weapons in Hi-Tech-Led Disruption: Cloud and Virtual Reality

Even as leaders in legacy companies dispute the necessity of digitalization and cloud-based platforms, disruptors from the hi-tech industry and start-ups operate with cloud-based technologies and platforms as a given.

In hi-tech, cloud development and support infrastructure is approved by the finance department in 90 percent of all cases without debate, whereas in non-hi-tech industries, finance is slow and resistant to these decisions (TGTS data).

How the Cloud Makes a Difference

Figure 13 shows a mapping of two type of cloud benefits studied in over five hundred companies. On the x-axis is the reduction of IT infrastructure costs, and the y-axis shows the solution acceleration benefits of the cloud. As the top-right quadrant of Figure 13 illustrates, enterprise-wide adoption of the cloud not only lowers infrastructure costs but also accelerates product and application development cycles. While companies in other industries debate whether there are true cost savings from cloud adoption, hi-tech is powered by a clear understanding of the true power of the cloud. The hi-tech industry does anything it can to accelerate its cycles and therefore treats engineering infrastructure as a commodity on which it should not waste any time. The result is that hi-tech reaps the cost and acceleration benefits of the cloud at a very different order of magnitude.

> The hi-tech industry does anything it can to accelerate its cycles and therefore treats engineering infrastructure as a commodity on which it should not waste any time.

FIGURE 13. 2019 INDUSTRY POSITIONING QUADRANT: CLOUD ADOPTION
BY HI-TECH

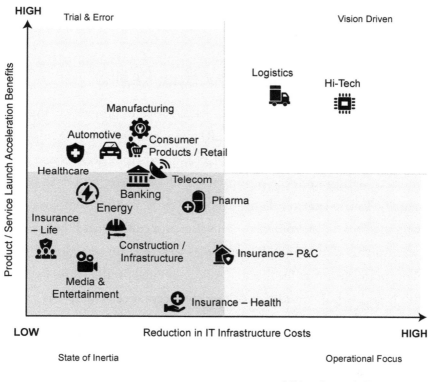

© Trianz Research (Trasers) 2021

Let us look at these benefits a bit more closely.

On-premise infrastructure deployment takes two to three months
in the models followed by most legacy companies. The cloud reduces
this to eight minutes or less.

"Agile and cloud-native" software development cycles followed
in hi-tech reduce the concept-to-release cycle time of solutions by 33
to 50 percent.

Cycle-time reduction: While a large company may take anywhere
from twelve to eighteen months to release a major customer platform

or product, a hi-tech company can deliver it in six to nine months.

IT Infrastructure and Operating Costs: By moving infrastructure to the cloud across the enterprise, tech companies save over 20 percent of their infrastructure costs- which is then invested into new areas.

The Use of Artificial and Virtual Reality

In addition to using the cloud at scale, hi-tech companies employ design thinking, artificial reality (AR) and virtual reality (VR), digital prototypes, and simulations. These techniques help hi-tech to visualize products, design multiple prototypes, and test them with customers virtually. Entire labs in Silicon Valley are dedicated for companies to bring in potential customers to test value propositions and the experience. All this allows hi-tech companies to select the best alternative, incorporate customer feedback, develop the final product, and launch with high level of confidence of market acceptance (Figure 14).

FIGURE 14. COMPONENTS OF DIGITAL DISRUPTION

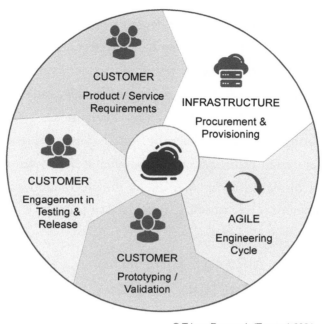

© Trianz Research (Trasers) 2021

The time spent and the process of engaging with customers has one big impact: the product or application being developed becomes almost entirely customer driven, strongly enhancing the probability it will be endorsed, adopted, and accepted by customers.

Net Effect of Cloud and Virtual Design Models

Clearly, the cloud and various virtual design models such as design thinking, AR, and VR reduce operating costs significantly when used at scale. There are two bigger impacts that these paradigms generate for the hi-tech industry. The first is an acceleration of the development cycles, due to which hi-tech can deliver technology solutions 30 to 50 percent faster than others.

So what do tech development teams do with the time saved? They spend it on ideating and engaging with customers. During these interactions, new ideas of value emerge that help hi-tech companies to elevate disruption to another level. They create early adopters and "champion customers" who are vested in the success of the product. They will support the product by buying, endorsing, and sharing their approval via word of mouth during a market launch.

This brings us to the final benefit from the large-scale use of cloud and virtual design techniques. It is a dramatic improvement in the probability of market acceptance due to the pre-validation, endorsement, and support of customers in the launch process.

Disney+: A Case Study in Counterdisruption

The concepts discussed in this chapter may come across as foreign, radical, or too distant. Unfortunately, they are not. This encroachment or disruption is taking place not only by large hi-tech players, but also by start-ups from within an industry. Traditional companies must move out of comfort zones, think beyond cash cows of the past, and embrace the process of disrupting themselves. The good news in the hi-tech model is that, with a sustained effort, it can be replicated. As Disney+, Target, Best Buy, and Walmart have shown, it is possible to replicate hi-tech's model of digital disruption. That is the central point behind this chapter.

By deploying the right data analytics systems, value proposition reinvention cycles, and cloud- and VR-driven acceleration, established companies can generate the same benefits. As you can see in the Disney+ case study next, companies have nothing to lose and everything to gain.

Return of the Jedi: The Success of Disney+

In a matter of three or four years, Disney implemented a strategy that began with understanding its customers (viewers of its movies, TV shows, theme parks, and ESPN sports channels); its first move was to create blockbuster superhero movies that appeal to the younger generation (Marvel and Pixar); it then acquired the Hulu channel and, in the process, its streaming capability. In the background, it brought all-digital content assets and a well-tested streaming platform under one organizational umbrella called Disney+. It then launched Disney+ with a massive advertising and promotion campaign across all TV and internet media platforms in November 2019.

The result? Within fourteen months and through the COVID pandemic, Disney+ garnered more than ninety-five million customers by 2021, even surpassing Netflix. Disney thus utilized every technique described in Rule #4, i.e., its rich brand, understanding of entertainment, and powerful industry presence, to disrupt its siloed entertainment model with a digital streaming model and strike back at the hi-tech industry—and so can you.

The COVID Effect on Rule #3

While COVID-19 has had a catastrophic effect on almost all industries, its effect on hi-tech is quite limited and, strangely, quite positive in most segments. The industry grew overall in 2020 as large software companies continued to see stable consumption of products and services—and a significant percentage of start-ups began showing strong revenue breakthroughs. While companies in other industries look forward to a "return" to normal, hi-tech will continue its growth march.

This contrasting growth scenario creates a potential mismatch between large traditional companies that have been vacillating about modernizing their products and services and the hi-tech industry. While one struggles with volatile revenues and financial and operational challenges, hi-tech gains a multitude of advantages in terms of customer intimacy (through continuous engagement and analytics), capital availability backed by a more tolerant investor base, more time to market, and technological knowledge to reinvent amid the dislocation in the industries it targets.

The Key Takeaway: for companies in traditional industries that are facing the threat of encroachment by the hi-tech industry, the challenge has grown immensely. What they can do to survive and compete, however, is to mimic and tailor the process of technology-led value proposition innovation. They need to focus even more on customers, retaining them as best they can while freeing up as much capital as possible for reinventing products and services with embedded technology—in the form-factor of the product, its functions, its usage, and its support. They need to analyze all data and keep improving iteratively. However, it must be a very fast race.

INSIST ON TECHNOLOGY-ENABLED VALUE PROPOSITIONS

Pervasiveness of Technology and Social Fragmentation

We all experience the pervasiveness of digital devices in our lives today. However, to understand their permanent impact on the social fabric and structures, let us go back to the 1970s. What people saw and how they communicated at that time was fundamentally different across the globe. Television, newspapers, and magazines were the only way to know what was happening in most parts of the world. During my youth in India, I remember my father asking me to read the *Indian Express*, our daily English newspaper aloud everyday so that I learned the language and spoke clearly. Radios and newspapers were how we got our news. Cinema and television were still a rare activity. There were no mobile phones, landlines were expensive and difficult to get, and people still traveled by train or bus.

Information was available through a limited set of avenues, and its consumption was often a group activity in the 1970s. There also was no real need to communicate beyond our immediate family or friends. There were no easy means to communicate, either.

Enter the 1980s. The sheer volume and variety of information exploded, and how people accessed and consumed it completely changed. We were introduced to IBM personal computers (1981), the Apple Macintosh (1984), the Microsoft PC (1984), and the public World Wide Web (1989). With the 1990s came commercial email, the first browser (1993), compact mobile phones, Cisco's high-speed IP networks, text messaging (late 1990s), and video-over-the-internet (late 1990s). The 2000s brought us the iPad and other tablets (2010). So what is my point?

Along the way, social structures, relationships, and the why, when, how, and with whom we communicate have fundamentally changed. You are now competing for your customer's mindshare in a highly fragmented and unstructured environment.

This fragmentation is growing in every segment, at the family or fundamental social unit level and at an individual level. If we received input from four major sources in the late 1970s—the daily newspaper or radio, family, school, and friends—today, the sources are infinite. Connected devices, content, and social media have ushered in this fragmentation at lightning speed compared with the cycles of social change we have historically experienced. People no longer communicate in the same manner with the same set patterns or even with the people you would expect them to communicate with, often conversing more with strangers online than they do with their own family and friends. When people are not communicating or working, they are often busy with content of various types. In the process, we lose the basic understanding of people and what is happening in minds that we once knew intimately. Let me relate a personal experience from my own home.

About four years ago, we found that our youngest son was spending a lot of time online, especially with gaming. There would be stretches of time where he was so engrossed in the online universe that he would not eat with us at the table. He was a freshman in high school, and although his grades at school were not affected, my wife was greatly upset by this pattern.

One Sunday morning, I sat him down and asked what was going on. His explanation was a revelation to both my wife and me. Apparently, he had developed a passion for gaming, not as a player, but as a developer. He had been writing "loops," or routines that were not part of the standard game, and making them available online. Gamers would download, incorporate these loops back into the original game, and play.

He also told me that he had a team of six other kids working with him. Two were from Boston, and one each from Indonesia, Netherlands, Turkey, and Bangladesh. He had developed a few loops that were downloaded more than a million times. He was also receiving royalties for his work and had already earned $500, which he deposited into his savings account.

Here we were, with so much change within the social unit of our own family and we did not know anything about it until we asked (needless to say, I stopped bothering my son further because I know he is productive, and he knows where to draw the line).

Today, the fundamental marketing assumptions of buyers and influencers are out the window. Businesses are struggling to keep pace with these changing behaviors in all industries, and the implications are massive. Once children are beyond ten years of age, parents can offer choices but they may not be the decision-makers. Children will decide what they will eat, wear, read, learn, how they play, or with whom they spend time. Schools will recommend but will not be prescriptive on what type of equipment or computer students should buy. Businesses may allow employees to bring their own devices but not control what devices their employees use for work and so on.

The consequence is a shift from established group or institutional social structures that we knew previously as buyers to a new set of decision-makers and processes.

If a team does not recognize these changes, they are not engaged with the right decision-makers. If they do not have the right message, their pitch will be lost in the digital cacophony around us.

> The consequence is a shift from established group or institutional social structures that we knew previously as buyers to a new set of decision-makers and processes.

At a time when companies are competing every minute and customer mindshare is fragmented, reactions will be hard to get.

Device-Driven Empowerment and the Rise of Individual Power

Generations of leaders in established businesses have grown up assuming that there is a clear need for their products and services, that they should target specific customer segments, and that they know how these customers prioritize, evaluate, and buy products and services. In other words, the previous business paradigm assumes, "I have a product that fulfills a need and I know my customers' purchasing habits." These assumptions are no longer true.

Let us dig a bit deeper and look at how the equation between a business and its customers has fundamentally changed. The truth is that by providing children as young as five years old with a device, we have set them on a path in which their minds develop semi-independently. They are dependent on their parents economically and socially and for their upbringing in a secure family structure. Outside of that, though, all bets are off.

Every individual now has their own mind, abilities, preferences, and attitudes. Some are social, while others are not. Some are hardworking, while others have an easygoing view of life. Some are confident, while others may lack confidence. Some are blessed with good health and strong economic situations, while many are not, and so on.

When people use their smart devices (whether that is a phone or a PC or a tablet, etc.), they are in their own cocoons, driven by their individual perspective and feelings.

One reason people are hooked on all sorts of content (be it reading, audio, video, games, or voice or video conversations) is because it empowers them to live, read, engage with, play with, and communicate with whomever, wherever, and whenever they like. The converse is also true—consumers hold the power to avoid whatever they want to.

In the Digital Age, customers similarly feel a sense of power and control over most aspects of their lives and regular routines. They will choose what they do with their time, and their beliefs will be shaped by their digital interactions. Their very definition of relationships will go through a change; their interactions will be remote and virtual and not just in the physical paradigm. The older paradigm is what most board members, CEOs, and executives have grown up with.

The COVID-19 pandemic has accelerated this trend and has also created a shift within this shift. The additional drivers of emotions are fear, loneliness, economic instability, etc. The directions this will take are yet unknown, but at a minimum, it will become even more difficult for companies to connect with the audiences they seek.

> Their very definition of relationships will go through a change; their interactions will be remote and virtual and not just in the physical paradigm. The older paradigm is what most board members, CEOs, and executives have grown up with.

The customer environment has thus shifted from predictable budgets, priorities, decision-makers, and process. Companies now face highly independent and "hard to read" customers with limited budgets and attention spans. These changes are triggered by digitalization and not by a tough recession. This shift raises three vital questions:

Does your product or service address a clear need, and does it fit into your clients' budgetary priorities?

Does your product or service provide fulfill those needs as quickly as possible?

How well does your product or service fit into customers' perspectives, values, and digital habits?

Your response to these three questions will play a critical role in the acceptance, usage, feedback, retention, or renewal of your products and services.

Aggregation of Value and Return on Time Investment (ROTI)

As the number and variety of content platforms grows, consumption thirst will increase sharply. Besides their normal work and social responsibilities, consumers will be occupied by conversations, social media, digital content, and various hobbies. They have little patience or time, and the company must work hard to position the value of its products or services correctly.

However, "value" is no longer defined as a financial return, utility, or association with a brand. Because consumers value their time and spare as little of it as possible, they will always maximize their return on time investment (ROTI). This means that products and services must appeal to customers by combining functions and accelerating interactions. They must deliver content quickly and easily and then set the user free to go back to their own priorities.

A Return on Time Invested (ROTI) is the ratio between value delivered by a particular function of a product or service and the time it takes. Customers' perception of value will be inversely proportional to their time spent using the product or service. The more a product or service delivers bundled value and the faster the user interactions, the higher its "Return on Time Invested" or ROTI. The higher the ROTI, the higher the customer satisfaction, retention, and referrals.

Let me illustrate this point through a familiar example. We discussed the mobile phone as an example of value aggregation. It performs all the tasks of physical devices, such as home phones, cameras, VCRs, gaming consoles, printers, scanners, projectors, and software applications. It has freed up the space taken up by these devices (an entire desk), and its weight (tens of pounds) has shrunk to a few ounces. It fits

> The more a product or service delivers bundled value and the faster the user interactions, the higher its "Return on Time Invested" or ROTI. The higher the ROTI, the higher the customer satisfaction, retention, and referrals.

into the palm of your hand and is quickly available for use twenty-four hours a day.

The smartphone has thus collapsed the time spent on using the features that old devices provided individually or collectively. It delivers the highest ROTI, and that is the simple reason people cannot let go of their phones day or night.

Fitting into the Digital Habits of Customers

Successful companies have invested in first decoding these changes, then understanding these trends, and have introduced products and services that map to the change. These can be captured in the form of a new digital habit model of customers (Figure 15).

FIGURE 15. NEW CUSTOMER DIGITAL HABIT MODEL

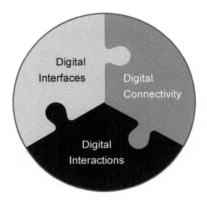

© Trianz Research (Trasers) 2021

Digital Interfaces

The first dimension of a customer's digital habit is a preference for modern form factor in products or services. These can be loosely labeled as "digital interfaces." Both B2B and B2C customers now look for a fit into a modern, highly digitalized look and feel that represents who they are or aspire to be. This should be intuitively clear in a B2C context where customers today simply will not buy things without a digital appeal. In the B2B context, customers will work with partners who "get it," who fit into that image, ecosystem, and a digital way of doing business. If a product or service does not provide that comfort and assurance, then B2B customers are unlikely to buy or continue buying.

Every successful product or service—from smartphones and films to gym equipment, clothes to cars, and travel to healthcare—now provides digital interfaces and form factors that appeal to customers. It begins with the online brochure and goes to the ordering experience. It extends to packaging and look and feel upon opening. It always makes them feel modern and stylish. Besides a cool look and feel, their usability is intuitive and obvious, often not requiring any detailed study by the customer. Therefore, customer expectations and habits have evolved at a lightning pace from utility to "cool digital or modern interfaces" and a company's products and services have to pass the "first look" test, i.e., appeal to a customer at first glance.

Digital Connectivity

The second aspect of customers' digital habits is a digital connectivity. It is often misunderstood that the product must have something to do with technology to begin with. It is important to understand the difference between a product being digitally connected and the customer being connected to a company and its products and services. In the former, customers expect products or service to be always connected to the internet. This will occur in most tangible, physical products with the idea that the customer's product is functioning well, usage is being tracked, and the company can proactively engage whenever necessary.

In the latter, when the product is in the "essential needs" category such as food or clothing or is a service, it is the company that is connected to the customer through apps. In this case, the company or product or service is continuously available to the customer should they choose to buy, upgrade, refresh, gift, or execute any other type of a transaction.

In both cases, the product or service must also be connected to other assets in their personal digital universe. For example, apps for buying groceries, making hotel reservations, keeping track of children, bank balances, monitoring health, and making appointments, etc., must fit into a customer's smartphone. Regardless of the business, if a company does not have apps for its customers, it is not in the digital game. Successful companies build cutting-edge product or service apps, ensure that they work on all the platforms, and constantly upgrade them with features. Not being connected to their universe is not cool.

Digital Interactions

Customer love products and services with intuitive digital interactions that bring all this together. They expect apps to figure them out, know their preferences, and constantly update them. They do not mind it if the apps track their usage but do mind if they track what else they do. They expect apps to provide freebies and always make them feel good. It does not matter what the industry is—its products must be as perpetually connected with customers as possible. This connectivity can happen through telematics (a concept that involves the use of IoT devices. They make hardware products just another IP or internet address). Translated into customer-speak, smooth digital interactions mean a higher ROTI.

All of this connectivity delivers data from customers—the new lifeblood of Digital Champions. While some companies have wrongfully utilized the data they gather, customers still like to interact digitally. The benefit to a company is that tracking usage data in all such digital interactions helps them to improve products, services, and experiences. And digital customer engagement, tracking behavior, usage, and feedback loops are the name of the game.

When a product or service fits into this digital habit model and delivers a high ROTI, it will be a win for customers. The company wins when customers win.

When it does not fit into any of these customer habits and ecosystems, a product or service will not succeed, no matter how hard a team has worked on developing it.

> When a product or service fits into this digital habit model and delivers a high ROTI, it will be a win for customers. The company wins when customers win.

The New Source of Customer Loyalty: Tech-Centric Products and Services

There was a time when consumers used to wait for established brand companies to announce new products or services and would even time their purchases accordingly. For example, a customer would time their car purchase based on the model year and available discounts, or they would wait for the big brand to announce a new TV model. Even when they would go to a store, walk around, and buy the product they needed, the journey began with the product category and the big brands. Well, not anymore.

New customer equations increasingly begin with the customer searching for value in products and services as opposed to beginning with a brand name and then being satisfied with its value.

Previously, prospects for a product or service could end up researching, finding, and evaluating a company's offering—all before it knew of their intent. Such actions by a prospect, called the "buyer's journey" in digital marketing parlance, are now happening digitally and privately and not physically (either through stores or by talking to someone in sales). One consequence of this shift is that when customers love a new product or service, their word of mouth translates into a "viral" behavior, taking sales through an exponential growth curve.

Conversely, when an existing brand does not fit into customers' digital habits or deliver a solid ROTI, it will fail. Its appeal will diminish, no matter how long it has been around or how ubiquitous its advertising. Iconic brands will become liabilities when a competitor overtakes them in its digital appeal to customers. If iconic brands are to succeed in this new technology and experience age, then they must discard their cultures of entitlement. They must lose their sense of having been "the standard," be willing to modernize, and develop understanding of their new customer base. This is best illustrated by the James Bond franchise, long considered the most successful movie franchise ever and still going strong after fifty years and twenty-five films. However, as the age of superheroes dawned, Bond began to appear increasingly remote and an icon of the past to the younger generation. The producers of the franchise did what any business is mortally scared to do: destroy everything that represented the "old" Bond and replace that with "cool" new models. That is why in the film *Skyfall,* Bond's childhood home, his iconic Aston Martin DB2 car, his vodka martini drink, and long-standing characters were replaced by much, much younger accessories and actors. *Skyfall* was executed to perfection and resonated with all generations, becoming the highest grossing Bond film ever, exceeding one billion dollars worldwide.

Not doing everything necessary indicates an insensitivity to changing customer behavior. And when a company doesn't care about their customers' new preferences, how can it possibly expect customer to care either? Customer behavior in the Digital Age is absolutely a case of "you reap what you sow."

Empowered customers will reciprocate exactly the way they are treated. The digital-savvy competitor is working hard to deliver products that fit into their habits and optimize their ROTI. They are continuously listening to feedback and improving the products and experiences. In the process, they end up creating a process of mutual vesting. Their customers will go out of their way to help them succeed.

Every company obviously wants to retain and grow the customer, and that occurs by fitting into their new digital habits. But given the premium on their time, customers do not want to go through yet another painful process of switching once they are happy with ROTI they get from a product. Successful companies use connectivity-based feedback to make steady improvements, which lead to higher customer satisfaction. Customers reward them for listening, and the companies endear themselves to their customers. This is one big reason why new digital brands command such high customer loyalty. Think about this— Peloton, Zoom, Square, Lyft, and Uber are less than ten years old.

If companies in nontech industries are to win they must develop technology-enabled

> If companies in nontech industries are to win they must develop technology-enabled products and services. They must adapt rapidly, deliver the highest ROTI in their industry, and fit into their customers' digital habits through endearing experiences.

products and services. They must adapt rapidly, deliver the highest ROTI in their industry, and fit into their customers' digital habits through endearing experiences.

Case Study: Peloton Interactive

A stunning example of delivering high ROTI and fitting into the digital habits of customers is Peloton, the exercise equipment company. The company was built on a single question: "Why would customers pay so much to go to a gym that they are highly unlikely to use?" In 2012, Peloton launched a stationary cycle that would help people connect with others and watch and learn about cycling and exercise.

The gym model was challenging because of the time it took away from normal life. Customers had to get up in the morning and squeeze out two hours to drive to the gym, find a spot to exercise, and get ready for work. If they exercised in the evening, the challenge would be the same, getting to the gym, exercising, and getting home late. If one happened to have a family, then squeezing in time was even more difficult.

With Peloton, the time customers spend on exercise is now elastic. On some days, they can exercise for a long time. On busy days, they can exercise for twenty minutes. They do not have to drive or find parking. The gym is right there at home.

In its first six years, Peloton grew from zero to about $400M in revenues. In the past few years, it built a bigger library of video classes, music, and more modern TV interfaces. The company really started catching up, growing from $432M in 2018 to $915M in 2019. Enter COVID, and gyms just closed across the world. Peloton grew by 110 percent to $1.86M in 2020.

Peloton is a picture-perfect case of delivering technology-enabled value propositions and ROTI that we have discussed in this chapter. It is also a prime example of a tech start-up transforming an industry business model. Peloton's loyal customers question the gym value proposition and show a cult-like following. Their feedback also helps Peloton to diversify its portfolio, thereby enhancing its customer base and revenues.

The COVID Effect on Rule #4

In a study done in March to April 2020 in the United States (i.e., right after the COVID-19 pandemic broke out), the consumption of online content from public sources and entertainment houses such as Netflix and Amazon Prime increased from 22 to 60 percent, ranging across various categories, such as games, videos, news, television, and music. Shopping for nonessential goods went up between 74 and 220 percent, depending on customer demographics and product categories. While there are demographic and geographic variations to the rise, the key point to note is that *all* this activity is happening through a device, not in person.

It is significant that these increased purchases of nonessential goods and services took place during a time of steep income drops. This kind of growth, therefore, would not be possible unless online shopping has attracted a brand-new set of customers, or in other words, we now have a larger tech-savvy population that digitally evaluates, compares, buys, receives, installs, and uses products.

Even though COVID-19 will eventually subside, this digital shift is likely to be a permanent habit for these people because of convenience, safety, and generally lower pricing.

The Key Takeaway: the beneficiaries of this trend very clearly are companies with a strong online presence, great products and services, and a digital appeal. Traditional companies must move very aggressively to rethink their value promise and embed technology in the form factor, delivery, installation, usage, sales, and support of their products and services. Otherwise, the gap with companies that are succeeding in the middle of COVID will only grow and soon become insurmountable.

RULE #5

BREAK FUNCTIONAL SILOS TO BECOME AN EXPERIENCE-DRIVEN ORGANIZATION

So far, we have discussed rules around customer centricity and the need to replace assumptions with data. We have talked about tech-led value propositions and disrupting from within before the hi-tech industry encroaches on the industry. Rule #5 addresses another key element of transitioning into the Digital Age. This is the removal of obstacles in an organization to exceed customer expectations.

As you begin transforming, your promises to *all* of your stakeholders changes dramatically. In the case of customers, you are making a new value promise in your products and services. To make inroads into customers, channel partners must sell more online. To deliver new features, engineering and manufacturing suppliers must deliver superior products. Delivering a new product or service, therefore, is not just a marketing or sales task. It involves multiple parties inside the organization.

Let us take the example of a company that produces toys for children. As part of its drive to transform, its team has made funda mental changes to two of its bestselling toys. It has introduced exciting features, digital interfaces, new content, and peer-to-peer connections.

What happens next?

Because of its brand and a great market launch, customers love the new toys and the company sees a sales spike. Existing customers also cannot wait to upgrade to the new product. To complicate matters,

---

Delivering a new product or service, therefore, is not just a marketing or sales task. It involves multiple parties inside the organization.

---

marketing informs everyone that the company is attracting customers in new demographic and geographic segments. The volumes are also expected to increase in the initial months.

In this example, the company seems to be perfectly set up for a huge win. But while everyone is rightfully celebrating, the game has only just started. It turns out that marketing was ahead of the game in building up the excitement. Technical support and services organization were not briefed, prepared, structured, or ready with new operating procedures. They had not yet built the systems necessary to capture customer data or identify and fix the underlying issues proactively. User issues begin to grow, customers begin posting bad reviews, the sales spike flattens, and numbers begin to decline. What just happened here?

The functions that deliver on the value promise in the toys—order fulfillment, services, digital content, and tech support—are different from those who make the promise—i.e., marketing and sales. They could not keep the new value promise as they did not understand what these promises are, train personnel, set up the new support services. The entire company did not see the customer life cycle as a series of connected experiences.

New Products and Services Set New Expectations with Customers

Most companies do not realize the extent to which changes to a product's value proposition create a new set of expectations of them—from both existing and new customers. Let us look at some Digital Age examples of value propositions in existing industries (Table 2).

TABLE 2. NEW VALUE PROPOSITIONS CREATE NEW CUSTOMER EXPECTATIONS—EXAMPLES

COMPANY	INDUSTRY	VALUE PROPOSITION	NEW CUSTOMER EXPECTATIONS
Airbnb		Book unique places (homes) to stay and things to do; value-based pricing	Service: Better locations and standards than hotels; same privacy and security Experience: App-based, fast, low-touch, all-digital
Lyft		Request a ride now	Service: Anytime, anywhere, always on time; clean cars, polite drivers, reliable and safe service Experience: App-based, fast, low/zero-touch, all-digital
Square		Accept every payment quickly, easily, and securely from anywhere	Product: Simplicity of use (plug-in payment system), instant transactions, lower costs. Experience: App-based, zero-touch, all-digital
Ally Bank		Your digital bank (online bank)	Service: Branchless banking, instant service, secure transactions, lower fees Experience: Zero-touch, app-based, all-digital
Heal		Schedule a doctor for a house calls 8:00. a.m.–8:00 p.m., seven days/ week; the doctor comes to you	Service: Convenience, no waiting, qualified doctors, digital prescriptions, reliable service Experience: Low-touch, app-based, all-digital

© Trianz 2020

Now ask yourself this: If your company were creating value propositions modeled on these factors, is the company's entire value chain—organizational structures, processes, systems, and measurement models—ready to deliver on that value proposition from one end to the other?

Expectations of value and experience emerge at the very beginning of the process and continue to the actual point of sale. If a company succeeds, all is well and good, and when expectations are not met, the customer cancels the purchase. The problem is that companies do not really "see" their customers and often do not realize where in the process they may be losing prospects. Drops occur when the product or service features do not meet the customer's expectations or the buying experience is not reassuring, smooth, and quick. For example:

A company launches a revolutionary light bulb. It has taken great pains to build an online presence and has launched successful campaigns and is seeing high traffic on its website. Prospects are thrilled at the idea of buying light bulbs that consume only 1 percent of energy as compared to other alternatives. But when they go to place an order, the web page asks them to either call a customer support number or send in their order via fax.

The customer experience in this situation just imploded. Customers expected to quickly order online and receive a cool new light bulb. But these expectations are shattered when they realized that orders have to be placed manually. Prospects abandon their intended purchases because no one really orders by fax anymore. The customer's ROTI also drastically worsened, and they found the proposition of a revolutionary bulb itself not very believable. To make matters worse, the company will not realize what is happening until it analyzes website data. Only after the company identifies that prospects are dropping off due to lack of an online order form will it make amends. By then, the company's credibility would have already taken a major hit, making it hard to mount a recovery.

Traditional Organizational Models Cannot Deliver Revolutionary Value Propositions

Large companies are broken down into business units that are further organized on a functional basis. These are "front office" functions, such as marketing, sales, and service. Then come the "mid-office" functions, such as R&D or product development, manufacturing, and supply chain. Finally come the back-office functions, such as finance, legal, HR, and procurement. Business plans are developed by the leadership and disseminated downward to each function. Each function then develops its own detailed plan to enable the business unit level plan.

Traditional organizational models rely on the concept of "specialization" by a function. Cross-functional coordination is ensured through business processes, strategic initiatives, matrix reporting, and decision-making. In this model, everyone assumes that responsibility for the customer is with marketing, sales, and service. Other functions are simply required to support the front office with policies, processes, or interventions in special situations.

In the digital world, however, expectations of value and experience change right from the customer's buying decision (Figure 16). The relationship cycle itself is now digital and customers expect the company to be proactive. They want the company to know their problems before they occur and

A tech-enabled product or service is essentially a new value promise. If the rest of the organization that delivers on that value promise isn't aligned, trained, or equipped, the entire customer experience breaks down. A perfectly designed product can thus become a total failure.

prevent them. "I don't want to be bothered" is the new baseline expectation as customers maximize their ROTI. This is why the hi-tech industry updates phones, PCs, gaming consoles, exercise machines, or even Tesla cars automatically and without causing inconvenience to users.

FIGURE 16. NEW CUSTOMER RELATIONSHIP CYCLE

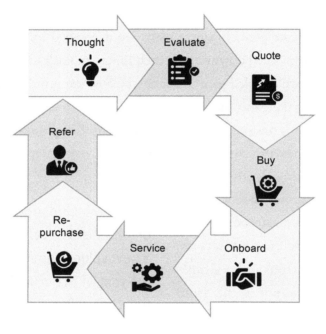

© Trianz Research (Trasers) 2021

In the new digital relationship cycle, customers do not care about an organization's structure. In fact, they do not even want to speak to anyone.

It is essential to understand that all customer expectations must be delivered from evaluations to a renewal and beyond as a single, connected chain, over and over and over. Everything must be proactive without a single word being spoken or an email sent.

In this new model, customers expect a low- to zero-touch experience every time they need a service, upgrade, or a reorder. Because delivering such an experience requires many functions, the disconnected and traditional organizational model does not work.

With new preferences and ever-increasing choices, customers possess the leverage in the Digital Age. Both new and existing customers are giving a company the opportunity to deliver on their expectations, to continuously prove itself, and to become a source for repeat purchasing, engagement, and service. Such expectations will also no longer be restricted to customers, and as industries evolve, they will become the norm from every stakeholder. Employees, suppliers, regulators, the influencers supporting the company—everyone wants to interact digitally. Period.

Providing digital experiences to all stakeholders is simply the right way to do business. It not only improves productivity, efficiency, and cost savings but also fits into the digital habits of stakeholders. It also provides invaluable data. If the COVID-19 pandemic has taught us one thing, it is that the sooner we digitalize the workplace, the better these expectations can be met and the more adaptive the organization becomes.

Enter the Experience-Driven Organization

In highly successful organizations, the functions involved in customer relationships go beyond marketing and sales. They include product development, which provides feature and value details to marketing and sales. Finance must integrate pricing and discounting rules into commerce engines. Legal must ensure that online contracts are available and integrated. Service must deliver and install products as promised and provide support. All of this must be done digitally, proactively, and in a manner convenient to customers.

Gone are the days of recorded messages: "If you would like to speak to someone in sales, press 1; if you would like to speak to service, press 2; if you would like to speak with billing, press 3." When you have a question that is outside of these realms, the recorded message says, "I'm sorry, but that option is not valid," and customers are left in the lurch.

Unlike ten years ago, customers do not want to be bounced across various parts of a company. The traditional notion of front, middle, or back office is therefore no longer valid, and every experience must be digital, seamless, and in real time. Therefore, every support function that provides an input or a decision in this relationship cycle must be connected digitally and in real time with functions that are customer facing.

Since expectations of digital interactions now extend to all stakeholders, i.e., the company's partners, suppliers, regulators, or employees and contractors, what is an organizational model for enabling continuous, connected, and consistent experiences? How can each function contribute to experiences while maintaining a focus on their larger role? How do we enable these functions—especially since their cultures are not customer-oriented intellectually and they lack the skills necessary? There are several ways to do this, but Figure 17 shows a concept that you can adapt to your company-specific situation.

FIGURE 17. STAKEHOLDER-EXPERIENCE-DRIVEN ORGANIZATION

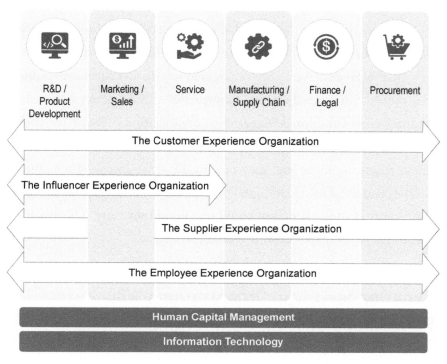

© Trianz Research (Trasers) 2021

The vertical towers represent some of the major functions in the enterprise. Human capital and IT are represented horizontally at the bottom, as they enable all other functions. In this organizational model, there are physical or virtual "experience organizations," with each covering major experiences for various audiences.

This model decouples conventional responsibilities of a function from the experience its stakeholders seek. The goal is to ensure that the function is able to continue with its normal tasks, such as strategy, planning, or operational execution. At the same time, there is a specialized focus on stakeholder experience. After all, it is unrealistic to assume that professionals in a function will be able to do both. For example, finance professionals in accounting, tax, risk management, or investing cannot be expected to understand "stakeholder experience." They are trained to think about revenue, profit, cash flows, risk, tax management, etc. "Experience" involves digitalizing of processes, automation, psychology, and visual aesthetics—these have nothing to do with finance.

In the Digital Age, experience delivery is technically complex and requires dedicated efforts. Companies will be better served by creating cross-functional "experience organizations" that have their own dedicated leadership, teams, digital technologies, and analytics. These teams could be mainly from the IT department. They could also be created by the chief digital officer (CDO). The traditional roles and processes of the function could remain as they were. This is what I would call the "experience-driven organization."

Experience-Driven Organizations Will Race Ahead of Their Competition

The benefits of an experience-driven organization are manifold. First and foremost, the company goes from a strictly transactional view to a life cycle relationship view. Second, it begins to deliver uniform experiences to all stakeholders. Third, the regular operational role of every function as it relates to planning, budgeting, managing key processes, reporting, and so on continues undistracted. But there is also a strategic benefit.

Experiences will become connected, continuous, and consistent as the company emerges as a digital brand. Experience-driven organizations under a common umbrella not only deliver consistent experiences but also share competencies, standards, technologies, and invaluable stakeholder data for further analysis.

These rules are all interlinked and the mastery of one rule affects another. For example, in Rule #3—replace assumptions with data analysis—we explored the need to harness data for developing priorities. This focus on experience helps to generate the data required to learn about stakeholder behaviors and expectations.

Successful companies analyze this data and reach the right conclusions and set up the next iteration correctly. Powered by the knowledge of what to do next, they achieve a higher velocity and stronger stakeholder relationships. With each successive iteration, they move away from the Digital Faultline and gain control over their destiny. As they refine value propositions and experiences, they eventually break away from competitors as well.

We will examine what "iterative strategy and execution" means in Rule #7.

The COVID Effect on Rule #5

As the COVID-19 crisis unfolded, business operations in most companies were seriously disrupted. A Trianz study in May 2020 on COVID-19 found that 90 percent of companies were unprepared to address operational challenges. This includes the best and most technologically savvy companies in the world, including those in IT services. We can only imagine the disruption in traditional companies with manual processes and requiring the physical presence of employees.

Let us review this from the perspective of customers and how their experiences were dislocated. Let us say you just bought an important healthcare product from your favorite company online. However, what do you do when you do not receive it as promised or if it arrives in a damaged condition? You call the customer service number or send an email but get no response. You wait for a day or two and try again without luck. When you do connect with someone, they cannot find your order. Your frustration mounts because your need was urgent, and you are concerned about the health issue and the money you have spent.

The issue finally gets resolved three to four weeks later. The simple question, however, is will you buy another product or service from that company ever again? Most likely, the answer is no. Will you switch to a new company that provides the same or a similar product but in a more reliable and consistent manner? The answer is most likely yes.

The Key Takeaway: COVID-19 has tested and broken operational continuity across most companies around the world—many of them large, multibillion-dollar corporations. In the process, it has exposed an inherent weakness of broken processes and siloed operations. While companies will get some latitude due to the COVID challenges, customers in the Digital Age will not be patient for long. They will move on to competitors who provide the same or better products or services with connected and reliable experiences.

TO BE AN EFFECTIVE BUSINESS LEADER, LEARN ABOUT DIGITAL TECHNOLOGIES

The Pervasiveness of Technology

Technology is everywhere, and "everybody knows that," as the GEICO commercial goes. We have talked about customers and their digital habits, data analysis, technology-centric value propositions, disruption by the hi-tech industry, and why it is important to disrupt yourself before hi-tech does it to you. Finally, we discussed the need to create an experience-driven organization by breaking functional silos.

As we can see, every aspect of the business environment is going to influenced by technology in some shape or form. Customers, partners, suppliers, employees, and even regulators now interact electronically or digitally. Leaders will need to visualize models, processes, and experiences with technology as a given. In front of their teams, IT counterparts, peers, or superiors, business leaders can no longer be bystanders or insulate themselves from technology. They can no longer give requirements to their IT department or expect them come up with solutions on their own.

Why Transformation Initiatives Fail: The Real Business–IT Alignment Gap

TGTS data points to several reasons why transformation initiatives fail. One of the top reasons is lack of alignment between business and IT leadership at a company or at a function level. Leaders of various business functions and the CIO are not aligned on the drivers, vision, priorities, technology selection, or the investments required.

The root causes of this misalignment are many, but it essentially boils down to this: the business side does not properly articulate what it wants to accomplish, and a lack of tech savvy does not help. Conversely, IT does not fully understand what is driving industry change or why business prioritizes things the way it does. In addition, IT may be taking a "technology will solve everything" approach.

Except for technology-intensive industries such as hi-tech, communications, entertainment, and banking, most leaders do not understand the fundamental digital technologies that are driving this revolution. Many are still in a denial or traditional mode, somehow expecting IT to deliver it all.

No matter whether this misalignment is occurring on the business side, IT side, or both, the teams are off to a bad start, and the initiatives will fail. The cost of failure is not the sunk financial costs but the lost window of opportunity.

As things get more and more challenging on the faultline and as the forces become stronger, the patience of boards, CEOs, and shareholders will begin to wear thin. "My IT department did not deliver" will no longer be an acceptable excuse. Every business leader, therefore, must learn about digital technologies and understand the pace and scale that is affecting their business.

Digital Technologies for Business Leaders to Focus On

In the old days, the tech landscape used to be simpler for business leaders to understand. A company had a customer relationship management (CRM) system, an enterprise resource planning (ERP) system, several custom applications time to deal with business-specific processes, and finally MS Office, email, etc. Leaders received their operational reports in a presentation or PDF. While there were many other aspects related to IT infrastructure, a business leader did not have to worry about them.

Today, there are myriad technologies covering experience, user interfaces, process automation, artificial intelligence, and analytics—just on the business side. The sheer cacophony of technology is overwhelming and omnipresent—on billboards, magazines, and websites. Click an advertisement on a website and it will chase you forever. This explosion of technology makes information discernment stressful. The challenge is even bigger for those who have not yet had a serious opportunity in their careers to learn about technology.

There are five major families that business leaders absolutely need to know about (Table 3). To be clear, leaders are not expected to be techies. However, given that they are taking their company across the Digital Faultline, they do need to become tech-savvy. They need to be able to judge, negotiate, decide, and monitor progress made by their business and IT teams.

TABLE 3. MAJOR FAMILIES OF ENTERPRISE DIGITAL TECHNOLOGIES

CATEGORY	FOCUS AREAS	KEY QUESTIONS
Cloud	Cloud infrastructure Data and analytics on cloud Business applications on cloud	What is your current state and what are the gaps with Digital Champions? Which providers understand your industry? What are the business benefits from using cloud for these areas? What do implementation cycles look like? What skills are required—on the business and IT sides—for deploying data, applications, or infrastructure layers?
Analytics	Data foundations Data lakes Data visualization Predictive analytics AI and Machine Learning (ML)	What is your current state and what are the gaps with Digital Champions? What is the sequence in which you should implement analytics? What platforms are the best fit for each layer—data foundations, data lakes, and data visualizations? What do implementation cycles look like? What skills are required—in business and in IT—for deploying these technology layers?
Digital	User experience (UX) and user interface (UI) Mobile apps Cloud-native applications Agile engineering and business collaboration Applications integration Remote apps management (post-COVID scenario)	What is your current state and what are the gaps with Digital Champions? Which of your applications can be migrated to the cloud? What can be built cloud-native? What platforms and techniques should you use to standardize UX and UI across your organization? What applications need to be integrated for providing seamless experiences? How do you move out of legacy applications management, reduce costs, and free up capital for growth initiatives?
Internet of Things	IoT devices IoT applications IoT networks IoT data analytics	What customer-facing or internal processes could use IoT? What competitive models are out there in your industry? What can you learn from other industries as far as using IoT?
Cybersecurity	Threat perceptions Types of security breaches Business risks from breaches Security monitoring	What is your security architecture from the perimeter to the core? What security considerations should be considered in applications and analytics development? What additional cloud security considerations should you be aware of? What should the business do to comply with security standards and requirements?

© Trianz 2020

Five Information Technology "To-Dos" for Business Leaders

Let us be clear: business leaders can no longer turn away from technology, because it permeates everything. Ultimately, leaders are accountable for delivering results. They increase their own and their team's tech savvy by doing the following:

- Internal technology roundtables. Request CIOs to organize industry- and business-specific technology roundtables within the company to foster learning.

- Mandate technology learning for your direct teams. Collaborate with IT counterparts and identify training courses that each of their direct team members would benefit from. Make this mandatory.

- Appoint business technology leaders. Identify a leader from within or hire a technology leader who is an expert in technology selection, deployment, and operations. This leader becomes the bridge between the team and IT.

- Design a process for business and IT collaboration. Design a process from concept to prioritization to tech selection and implementation so there is clear ownership and a process for decision-making.

- Take time to personally understand why digital technology rollouts succeed or fail. Ensure that those best practices are learned and adopted and that risks of failure are proactively monitored.

It is only a matter of time before understanding technology goes from being a preferred to a mandatory skill for every executive or leadership position on the business side of an enterprise.

Methodical Innovators are a step ahead and become shrewd investors in technology to accelerate their transition across the Digital Faultline.

The COVID Effect on Rule #6

One of the main factors driving the success of the 7 percent of Digital Champions is the degree of collaboration between business and IT. The model that showed the highest success rate was when business developed the vision, set the priorities, and program-managed the initiatives. There is an underlying competency cross-pollination in these Digital Champions: the business is technology savvy while IT understands what is driving business change—and they both respect and reinforce each other's roles.

COVID-19 has created other serious problems for technologically-challenged business leaders. Mass workforce reductions deprive them of skilled resources, and budget-slashing limits or removes their ability to hire external consultants to help them.

The Key Takeaway: at the end of the day, the responsibility and accountability to rethink, reimagine, and build new products or services—or reinvent business processes—lies with business executives.

Even prior to COVID-19, the lines between business and IT were rapidly becoming blurred. Post-COVID, they will have to produce these results in highly constrained resource environments and within very short windows of opportunity.

Now there is simply no way for business leaders to avoid technology or throw their requirements over the wall and wait for IT to deliver a solution. When business leaders are unable to keep up, CEOs will simply replace them with those who are tech savvy.

RULE #7

STRATEGIZE AND EXECUTE IN QUICK ITERATIONS

Traditional Linear Strategy and Execution Models Fall Short

Historically, business organizations have assumed that vision, strategy, and implementation are linear processes. Dedicated strategy teams develop a multiyear vision, priorities, and plans based on market opportunities and competitive dynamics. They then transition into implementation, usually with set milestones to be achieved by different teams. This type of approach is followed at the corporate level by business units and even by IT teams. I will call this the "linear model" of strategy and execution. Given everything we now know about the Faultline in digitalization overall, let's examine its validity in today's conditions (Figure 18).

FIGURE 18. ENVIRONMENT DRIVES EXECUTION PACE AND STYLE

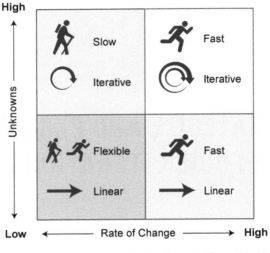

© Trianz Research (Trasers) 2021

When developing and executing a strategy, two dimensions play a critical role: the number of unknowns (which require assumptions) and the rate of industry change.

- **Quadrant 1.** When the unknowns are limited and the rate of change is slow, execution can and should be linear. This is because there is a good level of certainty of expected outcomes and a choice of fast or slow execution (lower-left quadrant of Figure 18).

- **Quadrant 2.** Similarly, when the unknowns are limited but the pace of change is fast, execution will be rapid but still linear. This is because there are few surprises along the way (lower-right quadrant).

- **Quadrant 3.** The Digital Faultline and the journey to get away from it occurs in an environment rife with unknowns. As discussed, these could be related to customers, products or services, business models, technology, or competition. When industry change is slow and unknowns are many (upper-left quadrant), execution can be slow, but the process must be iterative.

- **Quadrant 4.** By contrast, when the pace of change is rapid and the unknowns are many (upper-right quadrant), execution must be rapid and iterative.

Leaders must make this mental shift because the very success or failure of transformation heavily depends on the approach. When companies make big bets in the upper-right quadrant and drive a linear execution, they are bound to fail. The pace will be slow due to the scale of investment, team size, and the number of execution components. All this will be led by a decision-making process that essentially assumes a stable environment with few surprises. Therefore, when the external environment changes rapidly, the output will either miss the target or be obsolete. When they experience failure, they will not be able to react quickly due to the sheer pace of change.

> Given that digital transformations are fast-paced and with a high number of unknowns, a linear strategy and execution model is the recipe for failure.

The Unknowns in Digital Transformation

What are the unknowns on the Digital Faultline and during the crossing? While the nature of unknowns varies by industry and geography, broadly speaking, they can be categorized as follows:

- Customer or stakeholder unknowns. As discussed, customer behaviors are changing continuously, as do those of every stakeholder a company works with—whether they are employees, partners, suppliers, or influencers. The right balance between their definition of value and user experience is a continuously moving target.

- Competitive unknowns. As TGTS data shows, we are in the age of competitive paranoia. 50 percent of companies feel that their competitors are introducing products faster than they themselves are. These could also be new business models or process innovations. The gap between this perception and reality is hard to fathom, given that all players are strategizing at the same time. This aspect applies to all business functions and not just R&D, marketing, or sales. Everything is competitive and every function is changing.

- Unknown competitors. The previous case deals with what known competitors might do. However, a company is also up against unknown competitors who will be from hi-tech, adjacent industries, or start-ups in the industry. Innovations introduced by such competitors will likely be very disruptive and will not be visible until it is too late.

- Technology unknowns. Every endeavor in digital transformation has a technology component to it. As discussed in Part I, these technologies can emerge anywhere in the world. Product technologies can be highly disruptive. Internal business technologies will require complex integrations in its IT landscape. Put together, they create uncertainty and severely impact execution.

- Talent unknowns. Teams in an organization typically manage existing processes and IT applications. At the same time, the world around them is changing. New models and technologies are being introduced all the time. When the company chooses a modernization path, major skill gaps emerge and create execution uncertainty.

- Unknown pace of change. An industry's pace of change will be determined by its rate of technology adoption and customer acceptance of new value propositions. Given that all players in an industry are changing simultaneously, we can assume the pace is fast. But we have no certain way of knowing what it really is. So, there is always a danger of doing things either too fast or too slow, both of which are dangerous.

The hi-tech industry's culture of conceptualizing, developing, testing, and releasing products or services in an environment of high customer and technology uncertainty is based on the Agile engineering model. Although the term is very heavily IT-centric, the entire philosophy of agile strategies followed by leading hi-tech companies is derived from this. Its broader meaning is therefore applicable in the context of transformation strategy and execution. Here is some interesting history.

Spotlight: Agile Engineering

Along with the proliferation of personal computers in the 1990s came the proliferation of software. From email to complex business systems, there was an explosion in the sheer number of software applications. Soon, technology footprints across industries began to grow.

As the size of SW products and applications grew, the time to develop, implement, and utilize the SW fell out of sync with real-world business cycles. The SW industry had simply adapted delivery models used by HW and mechanical engineering industries. By the late 1990s, the gap between SW delivery and business change was such that by the time a solution reached users, their business had moved on. Clearly, the SW delivery model had become obsolete.

Leaders in the technology world soon became frustrated with the process. The overhead needed for the popular but linear (or "waterfall") method, which relies on heavy planning and documentation, was too much. There was no allowance for dynamism, uncertainty, or change in the business environment. Critical thinkers in the hi-tech industry were grappling with a massive problem at intellectual and applied levels. Jon Kern, an aerospace engineer in the 1990s, noted, "We were looking for something that was timelier and more responsive."

Out of this pain point was born the Agile software development model. A group led by Kern, Kent Beck, Mike Beedle, Arie van Bennekum, Alistair Cockburn, Ward Cunningham, and several others published the simple Agile Manifesto, which read: "We are uncovering better ways of developing software by doing it and helping others do it. Through this work we have come to value

Individuals and interactions over processes and tools

Working software over comprehensive documentation

Customer collaboration over contract negotiation

Responding to change over following a plan

That is, while there is value in the items on the right, we value the items on the left more."

This movement ultimately gave rise to a new technique called Agile software development. Agile breaks down the final output into smaller pieces, thus minimizing complex planning and design processes. Iterations, or sprints, are short (one to four weeks) involving business and IT teams simultaneously. At the end, an iteration, a working product, is demonstrated to stakeholders. A fully working product or new features are released as a result of multiple iterations.

Agile development was innovative since it considered uncertainties and unknowns that linear models did not. Of all the principles the group advocated, the last two, "Customer Collaboration" and "Responding to Change," were the most beneficial—especially when applied together. Collaborating with end-users automatically clarifies needs, reduces fuzziness, and gains higher acceptance. A response to change—whatever it maybe—forces continuous adaptation.

We have come a long way from the early 2000s. Business dynamics have only become more complex, with change occurring at an ever-increasing pace. The key point here is that elements from techniques such as Agile have become deeply ingrained in the tech industry all the way from software development to corporate strategy itself.

Successful Digital Transformations Are Iterative

In the military, there is a term used called "fluid targets." When the shape, location, direction, and resistance of a target are unclear, a conventional approach to engaging and winning will not work. One needs to do something different and pin down at least some of the variables and acquire the remainder of the target before fully engaging.

Conceptually, all digital transformation cycles eventually involve tech implementations and, hence, will suffer from the same issues the hi-tech industry saw in the 1990s. Given the number of unknowns and rapid rate of change in all industries, successful transformations are iterative. Initial phases are experimental, learning-oriented, and limited in scope. The output from these early iterations helps leaders and teams "pin down" some of the unknowns before going big.

Unlike linear or waterfall technology implementations, successful transformation cycles go through five major stages (Figure 19). The learning from each cycle sets up the next iteration of transformation. Let us see how Digital Champions progress through these cycles.

FIGURE 19. ITERATIVE TRANSFORMATION CYCLES

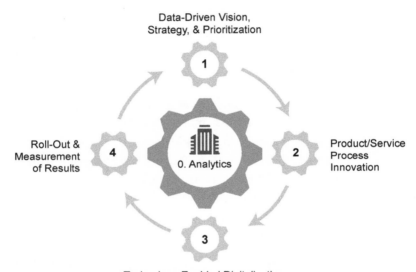

© Trianz Research (Trasers) 2021

- **Stage 0—Analysis.** Successful leaders begin with a data-driven analysis of the situation, irrespective of the core theme. Irrespective of whether it has to do with customers, competitors, employees, suppliers, they begin with data-driven insights. All of this helps them to understand the problem they are solving or the opportunity they aim to capture and develop clear goals.

- **Stage 1—Data-Driven Vision, Strategy, and Prioritization.** Successful leaders establish vision, concepts, strategies, and execution priorities. They also define what success or business impact from a minimal viable product or MVP means. The word "product" here is used loosely to include actual products, services, or operational capabilities. Leaders quantify intermediate and final outcomes using KPIs and measure performance throughout the execution cycle.

- **Stage 2—Product/Service Process Innovation.** A new value proposition, a business model, or a digital process takes shape. Digital experience, efficiency, and velocity goals are further crystallized. Successful teams use the concept of "product or service" in internal and customer-facing initiatives.

- **Stage 3—Technology-Enabled Execution.** Business and IT teams collaborate to bring innovations to life. Experiences are also reinvented and tested with external or internal customers. With Digital Champions, these cycles see the use of various virtualization techniques, such as AR/VR, to visualize products. Teams also gain validation from customers so that they do not venture too far without feedback. These internal or external customers continue to engage in the form of focus groups.

- **Stage 4: Rollout and Measurement of Results.** Teams finally roll out transformed products, services, models, and processes and begin to measure the results. Results can be both good and bad and it does not quite matter in the initial stages. The whole point is to understand what is working and what is not so that teams continue to fix what is not working well. This is the logic behind "fail early." A new set of measures or key digital performance indicators (KDPIs) must be framed to track results. Once leaders and teams develop this clarity, they deploy predictive dashboards.

By measuring the right metrics for a reasonable amount of time, successful teams can see what has worked in the iteration and what needs improvement. In the process, the unknowns will also surface, and teams will learn how to handle dynamic situations. These analyses help leaders formulate the objectives, scope, and timelines for the next iteration. Over a few iterations, they become more and more comfortable with the method and tools.

TECHNOLOGY DOES NOT MAKE TRANSFORMATIONS EFFECTIVE—PEOPLE DO!

If Technology Was the Solution, All Transformations Would Be Successful

Though companies around the world are investing heavily in technology, more than 90 percent of these technology initiatives do not produce the desired results. Data also show that no matter which business function is involved, the failure rate is consistent. There are several reasons for these failures, and we have covered some of them in previous chapters. Most leaders lack the understanding that transformations are about value propositions and experiences. They do not analyze data or approach initiatives comprehensively. Their efforts are often knee-jerk, piecemeal, and unsustainable.

Many companies turn to technology almost blindly to solve their problems. In fact, the hi-tech industry has marketed itself so well that people often fall into the trap of thinking that technology solves everything. Analysts predict that spending on digital transformations will exceed $2 trillion per year between 2021 and 2023. In their quest for modernization, companies spend tens of millions of dollars every year buying new software. From websites to internal applications, from data and analytics to AI and the cloud, investments are nonstop. Talk to a consulting firm and they will tell you what cool technologies to invest in, perhaps even before understanding the problem. But if technology solved all problems, then most IT initiatives should also be successful, right? Unfortunately, more than 90 percent of digital technology initiatives also fail to produce expected outcomes.

One big reason why most transformational initiatives fail is because their human dimension is neither fully understood nor does it get the attention it deserves. Conversely, when transformations become talent-driven, as is the case with Digital Champions, they guarantee success.

In this chapter, we see why investing a fraction of that capital in talent must come before investing in technology. We also see why such an investment must be continuous and not a one-time endeavor.

Recognizing the Most Important Asset in Transformations—People

TGTS data shows that leaders simply do not pay the required attention to their talent assets. Some think technology is the panacea, so they turn to consultants or software vendors to install it. They do not see the connection with their talent and do not involve their own teams in these implementations. Yet others believe the gap is so wide that they search for "digitally ready" talent, thus writing off their current talent even before the game starts. Then there are others who simply give up, thinking that employees are either not motivated or are plain unwilling to change.

A leader will not fail because his or her employees do not care or do not want to change. Digitalization, after all, is not the first technology-driven wave, and it certainly will not be the last. Macro-economic theory shows that each wave results in economic growth. As they adopt technology globally, companies eventually succeed, and this results in job creation. Economic data shows that unemployment in the US declined from about 10 percent in 2010 to 4.7 percent in 2019, even as tech-enabled productivity increased. Certainly, COVID will have a lasting effect on the economy, but most sectors will return to normalcy and historical employment levels will return.

To be clear, no one wants to fall behind during the transition, as that is a sure way of losing a well-paying job or a career. When asked about their job-related fears, employees may indicate the prospect of AI, an automated process, a robot, or a machine replacing them. A fear of the unknown, the unprecedented global scale and pace of change, and perhaps too much ill-founded internet content on the subject have fueled these fears. Such trepidation has always been there, but workforces do jump on board and transitions are successful, as data shows. Company culture, employee loyalty, and commitment have always helped organizations to change successfully.

In a Darwinian sense, self-preservation is one of the most fundamental reasons for high employee motivation in today's environment. COVID has shown clearly that business fortunes are tied to transforming the company or function quickly—now more than ever.

TGTS data shows that 80 percent of leaders do not recognize employees as their most fundamental asset. Some 90 percent of successful leaders do recognize this aspect quite clearly. They first understand the challenges from an employee perspective and then put in place a sound people strategy. They train, enable, and empower employees across the board, who then produce outstanding results on a sustained basis.

Fear, Anxiety, Confidence, and Commitment: Understanding Human Emotions in Transformations

Human behavior, emotions, and motivation levels change in a rather scientific way, not randomly. Everything is new to your teams—the technology, the change, and the iterative process of implementing new capabilities. As these cycles evolve, so too do emotions, confidence, commitment. The team and a leader's effectiveness also evolve, and the human factor ultimately plays a powerful role in success or failure. Figure 20 shows the evolution of emotions during digital iterations.

FIGURE 20. CHANGING EMOTIONS OF TEAMS IN DIGITAL ITERATIONS

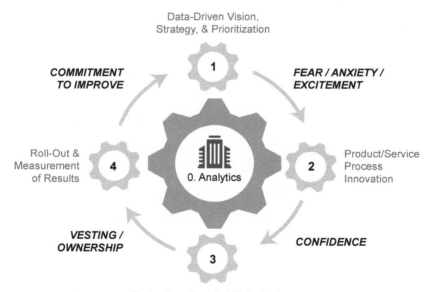

© Trianz Research (Trasers) 2021

The following shows how these emotions evolve with successful iterative cycle progress:

- Announcement of Vision, Strategy, and Priorities: At the launch of any new initiative, there is a mix of fear, anxiety, and excitement. Leaders communicate clearly and invest in training even before they start. As a result, employee emotions shift from fear to excitement. They feel included and know that their leaders want them to succeed individually and as a team.

- Product/Process Innovation: Training takes root, and employees apply learning in practice. As results begin to show, employees see how things really work and get a taste of success. Their confidence level grows in themselves and the initiative.

- Technology Implementation: As the implementations gain momentum, employees see everyone working equally hard. Leaders communicate regularly, emphasizing the importance of the initiative and appreciating everyone's efforts. In turn, this provides reassurance and creates an inherent vesting by employees in the success of the initiative.

- Rollout and Measurement: Everyone is happy with the team's achievements and their individual contribution. There is a sense of relief as everyone realizes that digitalization is not rocket science. The tension and drama are replaced with a sense of control and a realization of how business will be done going forward.

As a cycle transitions into the second iteration, employees are trained, ready, and know what needs to be done next. More importantly, they no longer fear new technology or even change itself. They are now deeply committed and want to ensure success. Each successful iteration strengthens confidence and creates a culture of commitment.

Transformations Need Many Smart Leaders

It is nearly impossible for any leader to single-handedly comprehend all the change that is taking place on the Digital Faultline. It is also difficult to develop strategies, direct implementations, monitor, and correct course. Therefore, the traditional hierarchical model of directive leadership fails when crossing the Digital Faultline. Whether they apply a sophisticated strategy or not, successful leaders succeed when they empower teams.

Successful leaders understand the importance of being at a higher level just to absorb, analyze, and predict change. But such a separation is only possible when the team below them is also capable. These leaders also know that it is neither possible nor right to hire in large numbers from the marketplace to accommodate necessary change. Such talent is neither readily available, nor does it bring institutional knowledge of a company that is required for rapid execution.

This takes us to one thing that successful leaders do extremely well. They develop the next level of leadership until every member of their direct team is smart and effective in their respective roles. They ensure that managers in their team understand the vision and priorities and lead with minimal hand-holding.

The management style of successful leaders is one of teaching, providing access to knowledge, empowering, and encouraging risk-taking. They allow team members to initially fail so that they learn from those failures. This process creates much-needed capacity that separates strategic thinking and execution. It also helps make leadership a force multiplier by increasing decision-making capacity. Put together, a trained and empowered second-level leadership team knows what it must do, takes the right decisions, and accelerates transformation.

Role-Based Training of Employees Is the Number One Determinant of Transformation Success

Successful leaders do not stop at building their next-level leadership. They continue the process until their extended teams are trained and regular communications are in place. TGTS data shows clearly that role-based training of employees is the number one driver of transformation success in every single industry, function, and role. Companies with high levels of success made the highest level of investment in training (Figure 21).

FIGURE 21. IMPACT OF TRAINING ON EFFECTIVENESS OF TRANSFORMATIONS

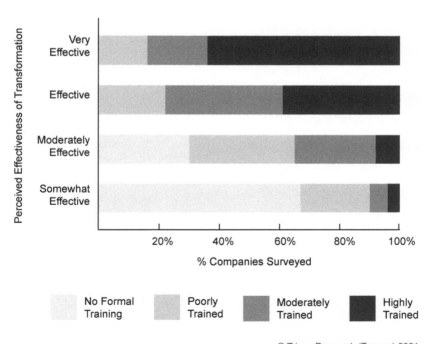

© Trianz Research (Trasers) 2021

Sadly, while training costs less than 5 percent of what a company typically spends on consultants, technologies, and implementations overall, only 30 percent of companies invest adequately in employee training. For legacy companies to cross the Digital Faultline successfully, this must change.

The global champions surveyed invest in role-specific training for their employees well before transformations begin. They make sure that their talent is more contextually aware and better prepared in advance of the transformations. They invest in training during and after digitalization to drive a culture of learning and to ensure that employees know how to execute their jobs in a changed context. Along the way, learning becomes a key cultural component in the organization.

> While training costs less than 5 percent of what a company typically spends on consultants, technologies, and implementations overall, only 30 percent of companies invest adequately in employee training. For legacy companies to cross the Digital Faultline successfully, this must change.

The hi-tech industry, which is often accused of evangelizing "job-replacing" technologies such as robotics, automation, and AI, is actually light-years ahead in understanding the concept of "talent powered transformations" (Figure 22).

TGTS data shows that the hi-tech industry is the number one investor in the training and development of its talent. It is the undisputed number one investor in the transformation of the human capital function overall. As the industry continuously invests in training its employees, hi-tech creates highly innovative digital workplaces and global cultures that do not simply accept but thrive on diversity and openness.

FIGURE 22. INDUSTRY POSITIONING IN HR

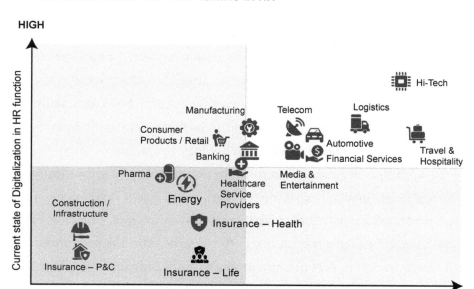

Survey Question: How mature is the use of analytics in the following human capital functions (X-Axis)? **Vs.** What percentage of your human capital processes given below are digitalized (Y-Axis)?

© Trianz Research (Trasers) 2021

It is essential that all leaders grasp this fundamental concept. Digital transformations are powered by people, not technology. Technology is not the "end," but merely a "means" to get to the real goal, which is to transform the business and change its outcomes. The more you empower your teams and make role-based digital-transformation training mandatory, the more successful you will be. The more HR invests in digitalizing the workplace and modernizing the culture, the faster you will cross the Digital Faultline.

The COVID Effect on Rule #8

By the end of 2020, COVID 19 had displaced nearly fifty million people from work, and the human dimension has seen the most visible impact of the pandemic. At least one-quarter of resulting layoffs were white-collar workers representing a wide variety of technological skills. These had suddenly been removed from in-flight transformation initiatives, projects, and business or technology operations.

Cliff-like revenue and profit drops and volatility have drastically affected the financial capability of companies. Every investment in transformational activities, investments in technologies, or hiring of specialist consultants is scrutinized. At the same time, the pressure on business leaders to perform and produce results only increases. There cannot be a more challenging "do more with less" environment than the one we currently face.

The Key Takeaway: TGTS data shows emphatically that "role-based training" is the number one driver of success for Digital Champion companies, proving that well-trained employees are more confident, vested, and committed to delivering results. Many data sources also tell us that training costs less than 5 percent of the capital spent on various outsourced initiatives. Given the paucity of resources during COVID-19 and the recessionary crisis, training is more vital than ever to maximize efficiency and output and drive success with the teams you already have.

RULE # 9

MEASURE KPIs AND DO NOT STOP AFTER CROSSING THE FAULTLINE

The Dizziness Effect in Digital Transformations

Consider the following—if you had to run a marathon with a group, which option would you choose: across the open countryside or in an enclosed stadium? Both approaches cover the same distance, albeit at different paces and in different environments.

Linear and milestone-based execution is like running in open country. It is slow-paced with static team structures and well-known decision-making procedures. Each milestone gives team members a sense of accomplishment. This method has matured over decades due to extensive practice, use of project management tools, and training. Still, the danger with linear executions is its disconnect with external uncertainties that make a team's output irrelevant or obsolete. Therefore, nice and familiar does not necessarily mean prompt and effective results.

While iterative digital strategies and execution is logical, the process is not easy. It does feel like running a marathon in a stadium.

Each cycle is exhausting due to the scorching pace and a lack of tangible results in the initial cycles. There is also fatigue that comes as certain activities are repeated with little change. Results are not visible until foundational activities are completed and execution matures.

The larger and more complex an initiative, the higher the potential for fatigue in early iterations. Leaders must be patient, set realistic expectations, and communicate with their teams frequently. They must surround themselves with team members who are equally smart and tenacious. Every progress must be tracked and every success must be celebrated!

How Do You Know When You Have Successfully Crossed the Digital Faultline?

Whether you have a small and localized or a large cross-functional initiative, how do you know that you are succeeding? What are the choices if you are not succeeding? What are the clearest signs that you have crossed the Digital Faultline? These are all very common questions during digital transformations.

Successful leaders visualize their future and business outcomes before change happens. They are clear about the broad themes, such as positioning, new business models, or growth strategies, right at the beginning. And they structure their initiatives to achieve that vision.

In his early years, the great Muhammad Ali was famous for predicting the round in which he would win a boxing bout. Media personalities, celebrities, and opponents found those predictions to be a sign of arrogance, comical, and Ali playing mind games. Ali was right twelve out of the fifteen times, and he went on to win the other three bouts as well within a round or two of his prediction. Under a caution from the boxing commission, he stopped making these predictions.

Why was he successful? He would train harder than anyone; he studied his opponents in great detail, contrary to his dismissive and belittling style of speaking. He would strategize with his trainers, he would practice his bouts, and on the final day, he would box exactly as he planned. The results were inevitable. Ali ended his career with six world heavyweight championships and was never beaten by the same opponent twice.

Digital transformation is not about painting a picture of the future alone. It is about knowing what specific business metrics must change because of the new approach or capability. These could be efficiency related, such as an improvement in the time to market and acceptance of a new product, or they could be financial, such as the growth of digital revenues and profit improvement. These could target stakeholder outcomes, such as satisfaction, productivity, retention, etc. Working backward, leaders define measurable KDPIs.

Just as with the fragrance of a great dish during cooking and before tasting, the success of a program also takes shape after a few iterations. Initial iterations only yield few results, but leaders do measure and communicate progress with teams. Big results eventually emerge with key metrics tipping in the right direction.

Whatever the scale of an initiative, there comes a tipping point where metrics clearly show what has been accomplished, what the trends are, and what needs to be done next. I call this critical milestone in the journey as the "point of digital convergence." That is when you begin to cross the Digital Faultline.

Whatever the scale of an initiative, there comes a tipping point where metrics clearly show what has been accomplished, what the trends are, and what needs to be done next. That is when you begin to cross the Digital Faultline.

Successful leaders guide their organizations to this milestone with data-driven strategies and iterative execution. They invest in teams and create a continuous learning environment. They reach this point with belief, tenacity, tracking progress, teamwork, and adjusting along the way. Let us look at this a bit more closely.

The Point of Digital Convergence (PDC)

The point of digital convergence (PDC) is characterized by seven key aspects coming together in a sharp alignment. This convergence begins to take shape when all the rules that successful leaders follow deliver expected outcomes. As initiatives progress, these outcomes influence each other positively. Figure 23 and the subsequent paragraphs explain PDC in greater detail.

FIGURE 23. POINT OF DIGITAL CONVERGENCE (PDC)

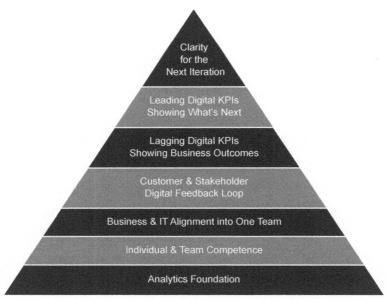

© Trianz Research (Trasers) 2021

- Analytics foundation. Data foundations begin to provide accurate insights about progress thus far. If leading KPIs are tracked, then insights about where they are headed become apparent.

- Individual and team competence. A team's competency becomes visible with the percentage of tasks they execute without a leader's involvement. Higher team competency means higher self-sufficiency and smooth execution. This leaves successful leaders with precious bandwidth for decision-making and planning what is next.

- Business and IT alignment into one team. Business and IT achieve strong mutual understanding and execute toward a shared vision and outcome. With the successful launch of products, services, or applications, failure rates and rework decrease.

- Customer and stakeholder digital feedback loop. New products, services, business models, and digital processes are more connected through applications. Such connections provide adoption and usage data that is used to predict future direction.

- Lagging digital KPIs showing business outcomes. Leaders and teams now start to see evidence of their success in the form of various lagging KPIs. If, for example, the HCM department in a company deploys a digital workplace, they will begin to see results such as the following:

  □ Percent of employees onboarding/using self-service

  □ percent of employees onboarded into digital performance management platforms

- □ percent of employees using various digital services within apps

- □ employee satisfaction stats and retention levels

- □ employee feedback and requests for new services and capabilities

- Leading digital KPIs showing what is next. Contrasted, leading KPIs give clues about what might happen. As examples: a few months of data about a new service begins to show increasing customer adoption, a particular employee portal sees a growing or declining trend, a particular knowledge app receives a lot of likes. Such leading indicators tell you where the trend lines are headed. Things that are going well are reinforced, what is on the borderline is adjusted, and what is not working is rebooted.

- Clarity on the next iteration. Finally, KPIs, analytics, research, other analyses, and new ideas from teams will tell leaders what they should be doing next. Internal unknowns, such as team competency levels in new technologies and methods, business, and IT partnership, etc., decrease. Governance mechanisms to address these on an ongoing basis fall in place. Finally, continuous research and data help the team address external unknowns.

Successful leaders and teams are no longer helpless on the Digital Faultline. They now have a firm grip on all the major parameters of the initiative, and they control the agenda for the next iteration rather than reacting to unknown or external forces.

All this occurs at Level 3 on the digital enterprise evolution model (Figure 6), when change becomes irreversible and you develop data-driven clarity about the next iteration. That is when you know you have crossed the Digital Faultline.

In aggregate, a team would have digitalized 40–50 percent of processes and collected and used stakeholder data for setting priorities and decision-making. The data now pulls you forward, and you are no longer having to push yourself or your organization.

Leaders Do Not Pause at the Crossing— There Is No Finish Line for Winners

As outlined, KPIs show both progress and adjustments required at the PDC. Digital Champions act on the insights generated by analytics to reinforce and accelerate what is working. If a certain action results in faster customer acquisition, they invest more in that strategy to increase the rate of acquisition. If certain services are more liked by employees in the digital workplace, they apply what they have learned to improve other services, and so on. In effect, KPIs guide teams to accelerate investments and course-correct across multiple areas that are not doing well.

Leaders in long-established companies have an additional challenge to overcome even when they reach the PDC. They will face a cultural recoil in the form of lobbying and gamesmanship by what can be called the "legacy forces." Here, groups representing past models, processes, technologies, and cultures will resist change. For example, in the case of Sears, there was the lobbying to keep retail stores to "protect" the physical brand. In the case of Kodak and Polaroid, it was the groups in film technology, production, and distribution who lobbied against a digital vision. In the case of Blockbuster, it was again about protecting the physical stores and resisting digital content. In so many established companies, this contest between past and future results in hesitation and inaction. It has sometimes even brought teams and progress to a grinding halt.

Leaders should never relent or slow down as the forces and lobbies that live in the past recoil and act with a strong force. Their intent is to keep the company and the proponents of the past safely in their comfort zone. The idea that a traditional and previously successful business model will do well is a delusion; while it provides an assurance of well-being in the short run, it is actually slowing the company down relative to competitors. If leaders do not let go of vestiges of the past forcefully, they will undo all progress made in reaching the PDC.

Let me illustrate this by way of an epiphany I had a few years ago.

I was in a small group of CEOs meeting with the president of one of the top two cloud providers in Seattle. In his introductory remarks, the president talked about the cloud, how its adoption was increasing, and how excited they were. He went on to provide a sneak preview of their future directions, proudly saying, "Last year we introduced five hundred and forty new services on our cloud platform." In other words, this cloud provider was introducing approximately two new services every working day to their customers.

I asked him how their customers could even possibly stabilize on a version of the cloud platform, much less absorb that pace of change. His response was stunning. He wryly answered, "What choice do they have, Sri?"

He was not being arrogant and explained it as follows. First, other cloud competitors were also introducing new features, so he had no choice but to do the same. Similarly, users of the cloud were rapidly adopting these new features, whether they came from this provider or another. His point, therefore, was that if they did not innovate rapidly, their competitors would overtake them. Similarly, if their customers did not adopt new features, their competitors in the industry would overtake them. In effect, none of the players had any choice but to absorb change and keep innovating.

If you do not transform continuously, the gap with competitors will only expand. If you transform at the same pace as they do, then you are just maintaining status quo. It is only when you transform faster than your competition that you get ahead.

The carousel of industry transformation will continue to revolve whether you are on it or not. Therefore, there is no finish line or a ribbon for successful companies when they cross the Digital Faultline. The game just elevates to a new level.

This is the realization of successful leaders and teams upon crossing the Digital Faultline. Along with confidence, success builds a certain toughness, aggressiveness, and directional determination. Leaders also know that such success cannot be let go of or things deteriorate rapidly. These are the reasons why they do not pause and their efforts are relentless—even after crossing the Digital Faultline.

> The carousel of industry transformation will continue to revolve whether you are on it or not. Therefore, there is no finish line or a ribbon for successful companies when they cross the Digital Faultline. The game just elevates to a new level.

BE AGGRESSIVE BUT SET REALISTIC STAKEHOLDER EXPECTATIONS

The Importance of Managing Expectations

The pressure on leaders to produce results only increases as digital transformations speed up. In public companies, restlessness from shareholders will flow to boards, CEOs, and the top management. Digital disruption does not distinguish between public or private companies. While these external pressures will be less visible in private companies, they will be as intense.

Leaders will be under the gun to deliver quickly, but at the same time, they cannot ignore the challenges we have discussed. The list of executives who set the wrong expectations by not being diligent or honest about what it takes is extensive. Once lost, trust and credibility are difficult to regain on the Digital Faultline.

Successful leaders assess their task thoroughly and set the right expectations from the get-go. They understand the underlying factors and set expectations after careful consideration. They know the importance of the trust and support of peers, their superiors, and their own personal credibility. Therefore, they rigorously map execution challenges and manage expectations around the timing of outcomes. In the process, they also ensure that these relationships get stronger as initiatives progress.

Rome Can Still Not Be Built in a Day— Successful Transformations Take Time

To better understand what it takes to transform an entire department or a company, let us look at some companies that were termed "legacy" but have now emerged as Digital Champions. Each of these companies is large and complex but also well entrenched and well resourced (Table 4). Let us review what their transformation was about and how much time it took for them to get out of the woods and into industry leadership.

TABLE 4. DIGITAL EVOLUTION OF GREAT BRANDS

COMPANY	INDUSTRY	START OF EVOLUTION	KEY DIGITAL INITIATIVES	KEY RESULTS
Lego		~2007	Movies, learning, gaming, customer-driven products	Considered "The Apple of Toys"; emerged from near bankruptcy to $13B in profit in 2018
The New York Times		~2011	Digital, crosswords, dynamic content, subscriptions	4M+ digital subscribers; $600M digital revenue
Disney Theme Parks		~2011	New website, MagicBand (for tickets), Wi-Fi, RFID	Over 20M users of MagicBand, 20%+ increase in park sales by 2014
Domino's Pizza		~2011	Digital apps; integration with Google, Facebook, Echo	Share price improvement from $3 to $211; market dominance
The Guardian		~2011	Digital-first, evening print, online contribution (not subscription)	150M viewers per month; 600,000+ paying members; 56% of revenue is digital; company profitability
Fidelity		~2015	Apps, blockchain, AI, digital assets, mobile, zero trading fees	Best online apps; asset growth to $7.6 trillion; revenue growth to $20B+; record profit

© Trianz 2020

None of these examples are from the hi-tech industry and therefore did not have any inherent advantage. Their industries have showed volatility, commoditization, and decline over the past decade. Lego, an iconic toymaker, was staring at bankruptcy. *The Guardian* and *The New York Times*, giants in journalism, saw advertising—their mainstay revenue—plummet to near zero. Fidelity, an established financial services company, barely survived the 2007 market crash and recession. Here are the common patterns.

Except for Domino's Pizza, none of these examples are from the hi-tech industry but were being encroached upon or disrupted by it.

They were all on the Digital Faultline, facing dire prospects in the near term. Yet each of them focused on the long term and developed strategies iteratively, executed tenaciously, and ended up becoming market leaders. Their models are now copied by others.

Throughout this process, management did not set aggressive expectations or make big proclamations. Instead, they focused on a practical vision and plan for digital transformation. They steadily made progress and allowed results to speak for themselves.

Even a hi-tech giant like Microsoft under the leadership of Satya Nadella took six years after their decline to come back as the American company with the highest market cap. It is clear from these examples that it takes three to five years to reach the PDC, cross the Digital Faultline, and become market leaders. Rome still cannot be built in a day.

Successful leaders set and manage expectations carefully even while aiming for audacious outcomes. The more results that stakeholders see, the more they start trusting the leadership and its decision-making. They believe that they will personally end up doing well and therefore put less pressure on leaders. Nevertheless, such a level of credibility must be earned.

Mapping Stakeholders, Impact, and Expectations

Managing expectations is a two-step process. First, successful leaders map targeted objectives and outcomes and list the major risks they face; second, they factor in these risks while estimating timelines and resources for executing an initiative. Sophisticated leaders go one step further. They see how an initiative's outcomes affect each stakeholder and carefully set expectations with them. They also monitor these risks to each stakeholder group's outcomes individually. Figure 24 shows the stakeholder framework.

FIGURE 24. A TRANSFORMATIONAL LEADER'S STAKEHOLDER FRAMEWORK

© Trianz Research (Trasers) 2021

Let us look at the process of mapping each stakeholder group, communicating, and mapping in successful initiatives:

- **The Leader:** They are their own most important audience and are deeply honest with themselves. They test their understanding with trusted team members and advisors and are realistic on what it takes to succeed.

- **The Team:** Successful leaders are transparent and communicate expectations and decision-making models clearly. They create an open culture and are accessible to their teams—especially when things do not go right.

- **Peers (in the Leadership Team):** Given that customer value and experience delivery involve others, they map peers whose help is required. They share plans, discuss mutual risks, communicate regularly, and help others whenever needed.

- **Superiors (Digital Champions):** Digital Champions are steadfast in their risk assessment. Knowing that messaging is not easy, they enlist help from peers and skillfully set expectations with superiors all the way to the CEO. As superiors see a steady stream of results and the positive impact on their own credibility, they become staunch supporters.

- **Customers and External Partners:** After aligning internal organizations, successful leaders set expectations with customers. They are measured and communicate only when and as needed in the early stages, and this increases as momentum is gained. However, good leaders never allow promises to get ahead of realistic possibilities. Trust and credibility automatically build as results come in.

Managing Board Members and Shareholder Expectations

Leaders in public companies face a final and more challenging set of stakeholders whose expectations must be managed. These are shareholders who expect both short- and long-term results at the same time. This is a topic that requires broader exploration, but here are some thoughts on what successful companies do.

If management in companies is just coming to grips with the

digital challenge, then boards and shareholders are even more distant. At the same time, shareholders are one of the most important and affected groups involved due to their investments into the company. As we have seen, many retail, consumer goods, hospitality, and fashion brands have perished or are seriously affected by this digital disruption. This story will soon play out in other industries as well. The larger the company, the bigger the impact and anxiety levels that the company's leadership must address.

It is easy to generate initial enthusiasm, rebrand the company, products, and services and project a digital look and feel. Shareholders, however, care about financial results and watch leading indicators every quarter. They track revenue growth, customer satisfaction, product launches, cost reductions, and so on. There is a dichotomy between shareholders' quarterly expectations and the time it takes to produce results (three to five years). This gap must be managed very carefully. Boards have an important role to play in smoothing these pressures so that management has adequate room to deliver results.

Historically, boards have represented shareholders and their interests. They govern various aspects such as strategy, finance and accounting, risk, compliance, executive compensation, and so on. In effect, the role of the board has been to act as a supervisor of the CEO and top management on behalf of shareholders.

In the Digital Age, boards must make a serious adjustment and become a two-way bridge as opposed to a one-way governance entity. They need to know enough about transformations to monitor CEOs and top management. At the same time, they need to help the leadership by way of shareholder communications and expectation management.

It is critical for chairpersons, CEOs, and CFOs to review and expand the structure and experience of their boards. Given the general lack of tech savvy at the board level, they will be well served by adding former IT and cybersecurity executives. They must also help board members engage directly with management. This will result in a better understanding of what digitalization means and what it takes to succeed.

Finally, the board, CEO, COO, CFO, and CIO of a company must develop a shared view of which outcomes will be achieved and when. A board must then help management communicate expectations through various forums to shareholder groups.

The COVID Effect on Rule #10

By now, the COVID effect on all stakeholders in a company—stakeholders, investors, lenders, employees and their families, partners, and suppliers—is quite clear. Stakeholders see a catastrophic erosion of value in their investments when companies fall behind; lenders face the prospect of defaults. Customers face disruption to deliveries and essential services. Partners and suppliers face the uncertainty of business from the company. And finally, employees must perform under tough new work-from-home conditions while homeschooling their children, taking care of the elderly, and postponing healthcare and other activities. Many have been let go by their employers.

Even though COVID may soon be brought under control, its macroeconomic effects will last at least a few years. The internal and external pressure to transform and perform will continue to be very intense such an environment.

The Key Takeaway: even in such a crisis, successful leaders cultivate an image of "quiet confidence." While they show empathy to everyone concerned, they are detached and intensely focused on their tasks, they prioritize objectively, they are thorough in their planning and evaluation of contingencies to not let the mission, superiors, or stake-holders down, and they are aggressive with their internal timelines.

In communicating these plans externally, however, they are cautious, outlining the conditions and risks while setting realistic expectations. These leaders enlist the support of their superiors, CEOs, and even board members when it comes to managing expectations properly.

What ultimately makes the difference in gaining control over expectations is the delivery of results and results alone. Once their audiences see these leaders succeed, shareholders begin to rally even more—providing a much-needed boost and commitment, thus setting up a cycle of sustained success. Until then, boards and management must work together to manage expectations.

PART III
THE PERSONA OF SUCCESSFUL LEADERS IN THE DIGITAL AGE

CHAPTER 1

THE LEADERSHIP PERSONA

A Continuously Evolving and Fluid Environment

Data shows that as the world begins to adapt to or get past the COVID pandemic, digitalization will only accelerate. Tech spending patterns also show that cloud adoption and investments into analytics (AI, ML, IoT, apps, etc.) are growing rapidly. All of this indicates that more companies are jumping onto the transformation train.

This triggers a new cycle of technology breakthroughs. In the discussion on hi-tech, we saw how the hi-tech industry innovates and introduces new technologies continuously. As more companies begin their journeys, the expanded uses of various technologies provide proof points to tech software and hardware companies on what works and does not. Ultimately, this leads to more innovation and even more disruptive breakthroughs (review Figure 6).

What these patterns imply in aggregate is that in the coming years, the forces acting on the Digital Faultline will become even more indiscriminate and destructive. In such an environment of continuous change, the size, financial strength, brand, and market position of a company will help it survive only for a limited time. As this change takes shape, what is a Level 4 or 5 digital maturity today will become a Level 1 or 2 tomorrow.

In this fluid, accelerating, and increasingly complex environment, leaders will have to address dual challenges in order to succeed. The first is to grasp the change all the way from its effects on their industry to their company and role. Besides expanding their own horizons, leaders must ensure that their teams learn as well.

The second is to change their style, since the management techniques we use today were built for a different, slower environment. The most fundamental management aspects of a business are its vision, mission, strategy, organizational structure, planning, execution, tracking and reporting, communications, and the human dimension. The governing rules for these elements were written decades ago and have not evolved much except for the tools used to manage. When the environment itself has changed, those management tools will not just be ineffective—they will systematically lead a company down the wrong path.

Who is responsible for revamping these management practices in a company? Its leaders are. Leaders in companies have the big task of understanding and changing themselves; transforming their teams and collaborating across the executive suite to gain alignment, better execution, and results.

A company will not succeed unless all of its leaders understand these two aspects: align and adopt new techniques that are relevant for the Digital Age. This is the reason why the degree of success and digital maturity of a company directly correlated to the digital IQ of its leadership.

Digital Transformation Begins with Personal Transformation

The rule that "technology does not power digital transformations—people do" applies to leaders more urgently than anyone else. In the inertia of fast-paced motion that management has become, we do not often pause to ask ourselves if what we are about to do is different in any way. Let us look at the themes that have emerged in our discussion thus far. They are uncertainties, unknowns, fast pace, iterative strategy and execution, failure followed by success. We also said this will be a long and tough journey requiring sustained efforts.

Why does this rule apply to leaders first? For the simple reason that if the leader does not "get it," then the team will not either. If the team does not get it, then they will not understand the tasks or outcomes and neither prioritize correctly nor know how to execute. The final result will not be positive.

Let us pause and ask some fundamental questions of ourselves. We must answer these questions patiently and systematically to change ourselves as leaders. Then comes the team and then comes transforming the organization—in that order.

- How is this digital transformation game different and what are the techniques?

- Are we as leaders mentally geared up to cross the Digital Faultline?

- Do we have a clear intent?

- What are the personality, leadership style, and execution methods required?

- How well prepared are my leaders as individuals and as a team to win this game?

The keyword is the "game." So, let us first look at the game of digital transformation from a leadership perspective.

Leadership in Digital Transformation

Consider the iterative process of transformation discussed earlier—Digital, Digital Transformation, and Business Transformation (review Figure 19). Ask yourself the following questions from a leadership perspective:

- Where do I, as the leader, fit in the iterative cycles of vision development, strategy, and execution?

- Am I outside the circle as an observer, having delegated or set expectations, or am I inside the circle working alongside my team?

- As the leader, what specific role do I play in each phase of strategy and execution?

- What decisions would I make in each step and what should my decision-making style be?

Both logically and intuitively, your position as the leader is in the center of the circle—not on the periphery and most certainly not outside of it. I say "logically" because, as a leader, you are the one setting the agenda for all the activity on the periphery. But it is also intuitive because every team on the periphery is only as clear or bewildered about this game as its leader is. It is intuitive because the best leaders know the importance of leading from the front in times of great uncertainty. In all great endeavors in human history, be it in exploration, science, or warfare, the most successful leaders are those who have led by example.

Even after I left the military, I often wondered why our senior officers and instructors always emphasized *leading from the front*. This was particularly true in the infantry and parachute regiments I served in. Leading from the front was the default assumption, but no one ever explained the logic behind it. It was an unquestioned tradition that had been inherited and followed dutifully for centuries; we were simply the next in line.

Many years later, I came to understand the reasoning behind the phrase. In any battle, each side has objectives, strategies, and plans. But when the contest begins and assumptions get tested, plans do not work exactly as expected. Often, neither you nor the team fully understand everything that is happening or what the outcome will be. A thorough "reading of the battle" is possible only after the initial rounds are fought. So the first steps you take and the first decisions you make will set the tone and direction for everyone behind you. When you move first as a leader and begin to succeed, you demonstrate courage that does not need explanation. You are effectively saying, "If I fail, I'll go down first. If I succeed, I'll carry all of you forward."

As a leader progresses in uncertain conditions, the team follows and becomes more comfortable in acting on directives and taking risks. They are less fearful of making mistakes and facing uncertainty. Sometimes they wait to follow until they see success taking shape, and sometimes they move proactively. Regardless, they soon realize that the risks that you personally are taking and your success affects the well-being of the entire team. When you communicate the progress and next steps clearly, the team also puts in extraordinary effort to ensure the mission's success. Everything begins to transition from being a leadership burden to a team effort. That is why you lead from the front and lead by example. They will follow.

During digital transformation, the leader must not be a spectator cheering from a distance. Rather, the leader is the captain of the team crossing the faultline, formulating strategy and leading from the front.

When the leader understands the game and learns and practices the right techniques, the team learns alongside. When the leader takes the steps, monitors, and communicates progress using these new techniques, the team responds without hesitation.

The most critical takeaway from this book is that to successfully lead your organization through digital transformation, you will need to systematically understand the game and quickly embrace the persona of successful leaders. This persona might be new and have many aspects that are acquired and perfected with practice. But all that your team will see is a strong leader.

What Exactly Is a Persona?

Leadership cultures and styles in only a few industries, such as hi-tech, media and entertainment, and telecom, have kept pace with today's swiftly changing business culture. This is because they lead in digitalization and are also drivers of change across the globe. The culture in these industries is highly adaptive and Darwinian in many ways. Generations of leaders have grown up with adaptability as a natural requirement and know that they are only as good as their pace. What comes naturally to leaders in these industries after four decades of evolution is quite foreign to others.

The grand canvas of change we have discussed, this continuous evolution, is difficult for anyone to fully comprehend. To become data-driven and adopt the 10 Rules of leadership overnight is not easy. But if leaders hope to protect their companies and win against the hi-tech industry, such a change in mindset and culture is vital. Leaders must adopt and innovate the persona and the methods of highly successful leaders.

The word "persona" has unfortunately become poorly understood. Knowing what it means will make the initial steps of personal change much easier. Dictonary.com cites various definitions used by Carl Jung, the famous Swiss psychiatrist of the nineteenth century. Jung describes "persona" as a "mask or façade presented to satisfy the demands of the situation or the environment and not representing the inner personality of the individual." Jung points out that such behaviors are often a mask to get through life whereas the inner identity may be quite different.

> If leaders hope to protect their companies and win against the hi-tech industry, such a change in mindset and culture is vital. Leaders must adopt and innovate the persona and the methods of highly successful leaders.

Let us apply Jung's concept of influences and resulting persona in the context of the forces of digitalization. If we now know that the rules that determine success are different from the ones we have traditionally followed, then why not proactively adopt a new persona today to ensure success tomorrow? Rather than allow these influences to shape us, why not decode this persona and ensure our business and personal success by using change as a lever?

The persona of a successful digital leader is an acquired set of analytical skills, decision-making rules, and communications styles. It is not necessary and probably not possible that an individual is born with all these skills.

Leadership Styles and Personalities: The Traditional View

To understand why leadership in the Digital Age is distinct, let us first consider the most common leadership styles (Table 5). There are many schools of thought regarding the number of leadership styles and persona, but for our discussion let us look at six leadership styles: democratic, autocratic, bureaucratic, transactional, transformative, and coaching. Each of them is unique.

TABLE 5. SIX TRADITIONAL LEADERSHIP STYLES: ELEMENTS, TRAITS, AND EXAMPLES

	LEADERSHIP		
	DEMOCRATIC	AUTOCRATIC	BUREAUCRATIC
Elements	Open, free-flowing, consensus-based	Top-down, concentrated decision-making, providing no options	Relying on structure, policies, and procedure
Personality traits	Tolerant, patient, group success-oriented, risk-averse	Top-down, concentrated decision-making, providing no options	Relying on structure, policies, and procedure
Fields and Environments	Creative fields (art, entertainment, design)	Fire, police departments	Governmental organizations Time-bound, turn-around situations and crisis management Armed forces, military dictatorships
Examples	Franklin Roosevelt (Hoover Dam) D. D. Eisenhower (US highway system) Warren Buffet (Berkshire Hathaway) Angela Merkel (chancellor of Germany)	Margaret Thatcher (British PM) Bill Gates (Microsoft) Martha Stewart (MS Living) Ridley Scott (director: *Alien, Blade Runner, Gladiator*) Lee Kuan Yew (first PM of Singapore)	Winston Churchill (British PM during WWII) Manmohan Singh (finance minister, PM of India) Woodrow Wilson (US president) Hideo Shima (Japan Railways)

STYLES		
TRANSACTIONAL	**TRANSFORMATIVE**	**COACHING STYLE**
Focused on individual events and transactions	Top-down vision, big-picture, game changer, knowing "the right thing to do"	Emphasizing strengths of individual members, diverse teams, specialized performances
Micromanagement, lacking big-picture thinking, insecure Negotiation skills	Visionary, charismatic, persuasive, motivator, team of followers	Guide, teacher, mentor, patient, allowing time for development
Transactional, repetitive businesses Sports and games Commodities, trading Mergers and acquisitions Trade deals	Dominant industrial companies undertaking M&A Technology-centric businesses Aerospace and defense Military Politics and government NGOs and Nonprofits Research	Start-ups in hi-tech and other industries Sports and games Newly formed management teams Creative fields (art, design, cinema)
Norman Schwarzkopf (US Army general, Persian Gulf War) Howard Schultz (Starbucks) Charles de Gaulle (French general and president) Joseph McCarthy (US senator)	Mahatma Gandhi (Father of India) Nelson Mandela (anti-Apartheid leader, president of South Africa) Martin Luther King, Jr. (civil rights leader) Coco Chanel (Chanel luxury goods) Jack Welch (General Electric) Steve Jobs (Apple)	Richard Branson (Virgin Group) Patricia Summit (U. of Tenn. women's basketball coach) Phil Jackson (coach, Chicago Bulls and LA Lakers) Juergen Klopp (coach, Liverpool Football Club)

© Trianz 2020

To be clear, there is no one right or wrong leadership style; different settings or situations require unique persona and styles that suit them. The life and times of the famous leaders identified in the table were all distinctive. These leaders successfully applied a leadership style in their specific contexts and situations. Similarly, the Digital Faultline presents an unprecedented and rapidly changing environment and also requires a particular style of leadership and orchestration.

A Quick Self-Assessment of Your Habitual Leadership Persona

Take the following simple quiz to see what your natural, or habitual, leadership style is. Note that this is not a detailed personality test by any means—it is simply designed to identify your natural style at a high level. This will help you to think about the changes required in the context of transformations.

Scenario: imagine that you are the vice president or general manager of service operations at a large company that provides manufacturing equipment for companies in various industries. Now answer the questions below. There are no right or wrong answers to any of these questions; they are simply indicative of personality types.

You and your team have been tasked with trying to find out why five major customers switched to a competitor; you need to report back with your findings in twenty-four hours.

○ A. I tell the team what I think based on my experience and ask them to put the report together.

○ B. I ask what each of them thinks and carefully consider their opinion as I build the report.

○ C. I ask them to review what happened with each of the most recent orders from these customers and build the report.

○ D. I know these customers are dissatisfied, so I outline my vision for what we should do to revive them and base the report on that.

○ E. I ask the team to analyze the customer service process followed for each of these customers and outline where things broke down so it can be included in the report.

The ideal makeup of my team is ...
(choose the one that best fits your opinion)

○ A. People who are personally loyal to me and will carry out my orders without question.

○ B. People who will get along with each other no matter what.

○ C. People who are exceptional at executing every single task that is given to them.

○ D. People who are critical thinkers and come up with innovative ideas whenever I need them.

○ E. People who are trained in our business model and processes and adhere to it with discipline.

		In developing a vision ... (choose the one that best describes your current process)
◯	A.	I always know more than the team and tell them what to do.
◯	B.	I consult with each member of the team and decide on a course that everyone is comfortable with.
◯	C.	I evaluate my team based on what each member did recently and define their next task in detail.
◯	D.	I question the status quo and outline the required changes very clearly.
◯	E.	I outline the business models and processes that need to improve and outline specific changes that I would like to see.

© Trianz 2020

ADD UP YOUR ANSWERS:

As:	Bs:	Cs:	Ds:	Es:

Depending on your answers, your habitual leadership style is as follows:

2 out of 3 As: Autocratic. You are likely to be a somewhat autocratic leader who relies on personal experience and judgment, often telling your team what to do.

2 out 3 Bs: Democratic. You are likely to be a highly democratic leader who keeps everyone's opinions in mind (in most situations) and builds consensus around decisions.

2 out of 3 Cs: Transactional. You are likely to monitor transactional excellence based on the belief that the better the execution of each transaction, the better the overall performance.

2 out of 3 Ds: Transformative. You are likely to look at almost everything through a transformational lens, often creating an exciting future vision and solutions to all present-day problems.

2 out of 3 Es: Bureaucratic. You are likely a believer in policies and procedures and feel that if everyone up and down the chain of command follows the right processes, then everything will be okay.

3 different letters: No consistent preference or style. You are likely to take a different approach depending on the situation and do not demonstrate any of these styles consistently.

The Transformative Style of Management and Its Shortcomings

At first glance, the transformational style of leadership stands out, appearing to be the style we need in the Digital Age. Indeed, the Digital Faultline is the ultimate transformational setting. There is a great deal of uncertainty. Customer behavior is constantly changing without directional clarity. New technologies emerge daily, and the rules of competition are continually being rewritten. The status quo is not working any more, and companies are confused; everyone is looking for answers.

Rising against similar situations, Gandhi championed Swaraj (home rule) and the Rev. Martin Luther King, Jr. gave his "I Have a Dream" speech. They visualized a world in which everyone is equal. In the 1980s, this was the environment of uncertainty and incoherent businesses confronting General Electric. That led Jack Welch, the newly appointed CEO of GE, to say, "GE shall only be in businesses where we're number one or two." Transformational leadership thus begins with a statement that aims to change the status quo. This leadership style is comprised of four key ingredients that deserve a closer look:

- Inspiration: A leader offers the vision or set of ideals to transform into a vastly better future state as they perceive it.

- Idealization: A leader walks the talk and becomes the role model for the team, stakeholders, and followers at large.

- Intellectual stimulation: The leader challenges, provokes, and moves people with powerful logic and mesmerizing articulation, sometimes involving even tens of millions of people.

- Individual consideration: The leader demonstrates a genuine concern for everyone. Each instance strengthens the leader's legend.

However, surprisingly, the traditional transformational leadership style falls short on the Digital Faultline. First, this style presumes that the leader's vision is correct. But we know that this transformative "vision" is made up of the leader's or a small team's own aspirations, intuition, assumptions, and logic. Second, it needs a highly intellectual, charismatic, and persuasive personality, which is not innate to many leaders. Third, time does not necessarily play a critical role for transformative leaders—they have plenty. The dynamics within their scenarios do not change as rapidly as they do today. Finally, their causes are against a status quo.

In contrast, change on the Digital Faultline is broad in scope, multifaceted, and dynamic. The digital battle is multilateral, or many competing against many. If a transformative leader's gut-instinct vision is proven wrong or impractical, course corrections are quite difficult. After all, everyone will have followed them expecting them to be right. Data as we know it today was either unavailable, inaccurate, or had to be manually collected. In the digital context, data is available in real time. Finally, the pace of the times in which some of these transformative leaders impacted the world was far slower. On the Digital Faultline, social structures, customer behavior, technology, and competition change rapidly and constantly. Failures leave leaders little or no room to maneuver and adjust their vision. A leader's failure is a competitor's success and vice versa.

It is these inadequacies that made me look at the data again. My goal was to see if there were minor refinements that could be made to this transformative persona or if there was an entirely new one being shaped, unbeknown to all of us.

It turns out there was: the Methodical Innovator.

CHAPTER 2

THE PERSONA OF THE METHODICAL INNOVATOR

Digital Transformation Demands Intelligence, Not Just Heroics

Since a persona is "a mask or façade an individual presents to satisfy the demands of a situation or the environment and not representing their inner personality," as Jung said, let us all understand the layers that make up the Methodical Innovator's persona. Figure 25 shows the dimensions of situational leadership and how they build on each other.

FIGURE 25. LEADERSHIP DIMENSIONS OF DIGITAL CHAMPIONS

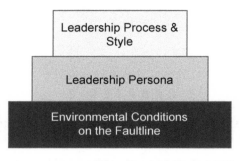

© Trianz Research (Trasers) 2021

An understanding of the environmental conditions spells out the particular persona that a leader must adopt. And to be successful, this leader must also adopt the process this persona would follow. We must first know the situation we aspire to change and then adapt accordingly.

Throughout Parts I and II, we discussed the Digital Faultline environment in detail. The essence from a leadership perspective is that it is a setting of chaos with many variables. Customer behavior, technologies, and traditional as well as new competitors, such as start-ups and hi-tech, all play a role. Not all of these disruptive forces are visible, and there are no set patterns as to how they manifest or the speed at which they move. On top of this, COVID-19 has only accelerated these dynamics and shortened the windows of opportunity for making a leap into the future. Clearly, the forces of change are massive and the resources and time available are scarce. These are the environmental conditions of the game of transformation.

Note that though most companies are spending a lot of money on transformations, only a small percentage are successful. If heroic efforts, motivational speeches, and incentives alone worked, then more companies would be succeeding. Such an approach, therefore, will tire you and your team but will not help you to win the battle of taking your organization across the faultline successfully. This battle requires intelligence—not superhuman efforts.

You are fighting to understand, control, and get ahead of a dynamic situation, not beat down an enemy. This is the time to think and act like the leader of a crisis management center. Leaders in such situations collect information and data. They piece together the puzzle; they visualize scenarios and ruthlessly prioritize their response. Finally, they orchestrate execution through the next layer of leadership while remaining strategic. This is the time to be John le Carré's George Smiley and not the Incredible Hulk.

Crossing the Digital Faultline is a game of calm and composed intelligence and smarts—not one of grandiose vision, bravado, soul-stirring speeches, or frittering away capital without proper prioritization or forethought.

Introducing the Persona of the Methodical Innovator

As we saw in the previous chapter, every style of leadership requires a strong array of skills and a foundational character. To understand the leadership persona required for succeeding in the Digital Age, we went back to the TGTS data. In that data, we reviewed the Digital Champions, the 7 percent of leaders who are successful out of the five thousand plus companies in the sample. These leaders demonstrate a unique set of traits and skills, attributes that can be categorized into strategic thinking, prioritization and planning, organization and execution, and their core character. From this, we abstracted a new persona that is unique: the Methodical Innovator.

What stands out in this persona is that every single layer has an embedded learning and practice of a particular method of doing things.

Nothing in this model is possible without developing and practicing a technique—even its character. This is the reason for calling this personality type the Methodical Innovator: one who relies on the method in each and every aspect of leadership and management (Figure 26).

FIGURE 26. METHODICAL INNOVATOR PERSONA

STRATEGIC THINKING	• Analytical, big-picture thinker • Data-driven decision maker • Visualizes digitalization outcomes before launching initiatives	• Creative, innovative risk-taker • Views digitalization as a continuous process, not an end state
PRIORITIZATION & PLANNING	• Data-driven decision-maker on priorities, structures, & technology • Adjusts and adapts to changing conditions	• Goes into details but does not micromanage • Takes logical risks wherever data is not available
ORGANIZATION & EXECUTION	• Ensures direct reports are better than self in roles • Empowers, but is demanding of teams • Measures outcomes with data & KPIs	• Invests heavily in digital training of extended teams • Monitors continuously; reviews rhythmically
CHARACTER	• Honest; leads by example • Great listener; no ego • Tenacious; never quits • Takes personal accountability for failure	• Precise communicator • Trusts people; verifies with data • Credits the team with success

© Trianz Research (Trasers) 2021

First and foremost, Methodical Innovators develop an extraordinary understanding of the situation at a big-picture level. They can connect the dots and boil down complex dynamics into simple, easy-to-understand root causes, dynamics, and impacts. They are intensely stakeholder-focused (i.e., if they are in marketing or sales, they are customer-focused; if they are in procurement, they are supplier-focused; if they are in HR, they are employee-focused, etc.).

Methodical Innovators analyze data across their ecosystems and develop their vision, strategy, and priorities based on these analyses. Given their focus on outcomes, they are not emotional or attached to the past. They are willing to let go of prior business models and processes if the analytics support doing so. Methodical Innovators visualize transformations in terms of quantifiable value and measurable outcomes for stakeholders.

> First and foremost, Methodical Innovators develop an extraordinary understanding of the situation at a big-picture level. They can connect the dots and boil down complex dynamics into simple, easy-to-understand root causes, dynamics, and impacts.

They are relentless executors who understand that this change is iterative. They are tenacious and exhibit patience through several iterations until results begin to show. At the same time, they underscore the urgency of getting things done since they know time is not on their side. As demanding as they are, they also realize that success is all about aligning and nurturing talent. Thus, they are people-oriented and invest heavily in preparing their talent.

The common aspect in the top three categories of Figure 26 is that Methodical Innovators are data-driven. Whether the task involves their vision, priorities, strategies, evaluation of talent, monitoring of progress, or planning future iterations, they base their decisions on data.

Character and the Power of Saying, "I Don't Know"

The foundational element of the Methodical Innovator persona is character. While leadership skills, experience, ambition, drive, and motivational abilities are essential, what defines Methodical Innovators is character. Character has several elements, such as leading by example, honesty, forthrightness, and tenacity. Lack of ego and commitment to honesty set the tone for how a team behaves and make the ultimate difference between success or failure.

Methodical Innovators practice a "no ego" approach. When the scale of the problem, the power of the forces, and what they do not know dawns on them, they quickly build a team around them, each member who is more expert than the leader in their respective fields. These leaders surround themselves with experienced advisors and professionals who are always available.

It is incredibly hard for any leader to say, "I don't know" in the corporate world. There is fear of being branded as ignorant, of being behind the curve, or of not being effective. A large percentage of leaders choose the tactics of ignoring, deflecting, or deferring problems. Many pose as if they know what is going on while simply buying time and failing to manage a situation.

In the Digital Age, "you can run, but you cannot hide" from what you do not know. The Digital Faultline quickly exposes pretension.

At the very core of a successful leader's character is inherent honesty. For more than a hundred years, studies have shown that the most important and admired quality in leaders is honesty. While we tend to think of honesty in transactions with others, Methodical Innovators are, first and foremost, honest with themselves. In an environment of unknown forces, dynamics, pace, and outcomes, they realize the importance of knowing what they do not know.

In acknowledging what they do not know, they begin the process of personal transformation.

From my career as an officer in the Indian Army to being a CEO today, quickly acknowledging what I do not know has always worked well. In the military, an officer's responsibilities go far beyond oneself. They encompass the safety and well-being of the troops under their command, the success of their own and associated missions. Poorly planned missions often fail, put lives at risk, and compromise succeeding operations. And the responsibility for failure is always with the officer in charge.

> In the Digital Age, "you can run, but you cannot hide" from what you do not know. The Digital Faultline quickly exposes pretension. At the very core of a successful leader's character is inherent honesty.

The very nature of military operations is that one never has enough information when planning—or enough time during execution of those plans. This dynamic of what you do not know is always present. The importance of admitting what you do not know can be illustrated by a story from my very first year as a commissioned officer in an infantry battalion.

We were part of a mountain division and were running practice drills for certain operations. As the commander of a company (one of the subunits in a battalion), I had to put together a plan and brief my company of twelve noncommissioned officers (noncoms) and one hundred and twenty troops. Having just returned from a training course for company commanders, I was eager to apply what I had learned.

We were given the task of capturing a hill feature, which required us to march about fifteen miles (twenty-five kilometers) through the night and assault at dawn in coordination with other units.

I drew up the plan, chalked our game plan on a large canvas map, got all the noncoms together, and began my briefing. About halfway through the briefing, the senior-most noncom abruptly called for a break and dismissed everyone. He had decades of experience, as evidenced by his gray hair and face full of battle scars. Having interrupted my briefing, he turned toward me, took a piece of chalk, and started drawing lines on the map to show me how our team would be walking into a trap, how we could come under friendly fire, how many troops would be killed, and why the mission would fail completely. He then went on to show me an alternate route to get to the destination that was tougher but safer.

I will never forget his comment: "Sir, I know you are an officer but remember this: when you don't know, ask. But never draw up or communicate a plan based on incomplete information or flawed assumptions. It will only lead to casualties and failures." We then reworked the plan, brought everyone back to the briefing, went through rehearsals, and executed the drill successfully.

The dynamics and responsibilities of leaders in an uncertain corporate environment are no different from those in military battles in terms of intensity and the impact on stakeholders. As a leader, if you acknowledge that you do not know or have all the necessary facts and information, you are being honest—and can focus on winning by overcoming uncertainties. Because of this, your team will succeed with minimal casualties. That is the power of saying "I don't know."

When leaders acknowledge they do not know something and make it their business to find out, the dynamics within their team change instantly. Why? Honesty is the #1 leadership quality from a team point of view. When leaders are honest about the challenge, everyone steps up and the phrase "We're in it together" rings true.

All stakeholder groups in a transformation want leaders to win. When a company has been good to its customers, they want you to succeed. The careers of your team are in your hands. You play a role in the success of the CEO and the management team and the outcomes affecting shareholders. Every stakeholder wants and needs you to succeed. Of course, your own career, reputation, and future are also at stake, and so success is vital to you as well. This realization drives the behavior of leaders in successful companies— they cooperate, help each other, and drive change together.

"I don't know yet, but I will make it my business to know" is not an expression of ignorance,

> When leaders acknowledge they do not know something and make it their business to find out, the dynamics within their team change instantly. Why? Honesty is the #1 leadership quality from a team point of view. When leaders are honest about the challenge, everyone steps up and the phrase "We're in it together" rings true.

but a rallying point among teams. It is also a straightforward way of removing unnecessary pressure on yourself and makes knowledge everyone's business.

Ignorance, pretense, and deflections are symptoms of a culture— and the more a leader tries to pretend their way out, the stronger such a culture grows. These symptoms also breed fear, insecurity, and mistrust among teams. Conversely, openness, and honesty change the focus from not knowing to "I'll break down the problem, I will understand the causes, and I will find out the answers." This is an action-oriented response.

This honest, almost vulnerable, acknowledgment becomes a pivotal moment. A good, loyal team knows what is at stake and will help you to get necessary answers. People are vitalized, the unknown is mapped out, the wheels of intelligence-gathering begin to roll, everyone chips in, and information starts amassing. Step by step, the leader now knows what they need for everyone's success.

Such a culture can be built by emphasizing honesty as a core value. It can also be created by a process that Methodical Innovators follow. Having a method removes the equation of emotions and fears and forces teams into action.

Leadership as a Methodical Process— The CCACC Framework

Thus far, we have examined the environment on the Digital Faultline and its influence on the persona of Methodical Innovators. We have also taken a closer look at the layers of this persona in terms of strategic thinking, planning and organization, and execution. Finally, we have looked at the underpinning character elements that constantly reinforce this persona. Throughout this discussion, I have maintained that leaders in the Digital Age will be made, not born.

No one can be born with the full arsenal of leadership traits and skills required to be successful in the Digital Age. But how do Methodical Innovators develop this persona and style?

Growing up, we were taught about leadership through a variety of frames, figures of speech, images, and stereotypes of heroism. We learned about values such as honesty, bravery, risk-taking, sacrifice, and perseverance.

We study strategy, organizational theory, and techniques to inspire others. However, we are never taught about leadership as a process, as a method, or as a skill acquired in uncertain environments.

TGTS data shows that Methodical Innovators develop a certain process that is eventually tailored for any uncertainty. In abstracting this process into a framework, I have relied on TGTS data as well as techniques used in the military. In broad strokes, the process consists of five major stages of personal transformation, sustained action, and habit formation: Confront, Comprehend, Accept, Commit, and Continue. I call this CCACC in short.

> No one can be born with the full arsenal of leadership traits and skills required to be successful in the Digital Age. But how do Methodical Innovators develop this persona and style?

In each stage of CCACC, these leaders ask themselves key questions repeatedly until things become increasingly clearer. Their actions and success in one stage lead them to the next until they do all this in a natural rhythm and ensure that their teams do so as well. Let us look at these stages and the high-level questions that arise in their progression (Table 6).

TABLE 6. CCACC FRAMEWORK AND KEY QUESTIONS FOR EACH STAGE

STAGE	KEY QUESTIONS
CONFRONT	Am I confronting the realities of change as they relate to my industry, company, and role honestly, completely, and without fear or hesitation?
COMPREHEND	Am I understanding this change from a big-picture, holistic perspective? Am I understanding its specific implications for my company, my role, and my team?
ACCEPT	Am I ready to acknowledge the change and its impact that the data is indicating without bias or hesitation, being defensive, or trying to wish it away?
COMMIT	Have I developed my vision and priorities based on an objective and unbiased analysis of underlying data? Am I ready to commit to the actions necessary and take the initial steps in the journey across the Digital Faultline?
CONTINUE	Do I have the right team, who can understand and execute the strategy? Do I have the resources and willingness to sustain my actions beyond the initial steps that I will take?

© Trianz 2020

Methodical Innovators ask themselves these CCACC questions and use derived data-driven insights. The answers that emerge demand certain follow-on actions that force leaders to extend their vision to their leadership teams and their organizations. This symbolizes a shift from leadership as we know to a more fact-based, data-driven approach. This will be a big change for leaders whose styles are more instinctive, democratic, opinion-based, or hierarchical. They are simply not used to looking at the world through the lens of data or viewing leadership as a method.

Let us say a company has three products, A, B, and C, with A being the historic leader in the portfolio. As part of their transformation initiative, the team analyzes customer behaviors. The insights show that A may be flat or declining in revenue over the next few years. However, C has the potential to replace A. Although C is only a small percentage of overall revenue, it is showing high growth, acceptance, ease of selling, and service margins. A normal leader might think of A as a cash cow, its sales making everything predictable, and, of course, generating most of the bonuses for everyone. Hence, it must be defended while B and C continue to grow.

Methodical Innovators will see the sustained customer preference for C. If the potential is clear, they will ask how the sales of C can be accelerated. They will also ask how A can be defended for as long as possible. Finally, the Methodical Innovator will tie performance measurements and bonuses to the success and acceleration of C rather than to the defense of A because the data says so.

Methodical Innovators use data-driven insights to understand and then make detached decisions during strategy and execution.

Here is a brief description of the CCACC framework and how Methodical Innovators go deliberately from one stage to another. You will see that all the 10 Rules we discussed are central to this framework of their methods.

1. **CONFRONT the change.** The scope, velocity, and quantum of change can be so daunting that many leaders may "freeze." However, the first thing to remember is that we humans created all things digital. The Digital Age is neither superior nor bigger than us. Methodical Innovators do not brood, develop a victim mentality, or keep asking why. They make a decision to confront the change head-on. They begin to gather data, accrue knowledge of the subject, and size up the challenge of digital transformation.

2. **COMPREHEND the strategic frame of reference and its implications.** In simple terms, a frame of reference is a proper classification and listing of facts, constants, variables, and trends in a given situation. Its purpose is to get everyone involved—

regardless of their knowledge and experience—on the same page as quickly as possible. It eliminates confusion and the debates on facts and foundational definitions. The bigger and more complex the situation, the more rigorous it must be.

Methodical Innovators paint the full picture of transformation at an industry, company, and task level. As far as possible, they do this using data and make minimal assumptions to eliminate biases. The more a frame of reference is based on facts, the more effective it is. Methodical leaders first focus on interconnections across the enterprise and understand the "transformation arena" and its rules of play. As a result, their teams and peers better comprehend the situation.

3. **ACCEPT the reality of change.** Procrastination in any form—denial, delays, or wishing things away—will only make the challenge of transformation harder. We have discussed the notion of windows of opportunity or windows of crisis, so it is important to move before it is too late. It is critical to get into the game before competitors and disruptors get too far and the tide cannot be turned anymore.

Rather than question its validity or imagine that their company is immune, Methodical Innovators accept that change is real. They move from "wait and see" into the realm of a "if this, then what" mindset. They use data-driven analysis to minimizes biases, emotions, and individual preferences. They build consensus and align their own leaders, peers, and teams quickly.

4. **COMMIT to act after data-driven strategy development and planning.** A good strategy is a must-have in any environment. But Methodical Innovators develop and articulate

their strategy with facts and minimal assumptions. These determine strategic objectives and priorities. These objectives then determine what the strategy should be. This decides whether to defend, improve, or change the game entirely through disruption.

The average company struggles with the use of data and making timely decisions and commitments to action. In a strange way, the clear impact of COVID on business has made developing a sense of urgency much easier. Methodical Innovators commit to action and deprioritize other things.

But what is the commitment for? As discussed throughout the book, Methodical Innovators break down ambitions into smaller milestones. Their goals are to regain control, i.e., cross the Digital Faultline, demonstrate success, and know that they are heading in the right direction.

5. **CONTINUE to sustain.** The first breakthrough that Methodical Innovators will achieve is not a complete transformation. It is the crossing of the Digital Faultline. When crossing the faultline, a team reaches a "safe zone" of sorts and is no longer dealing with the faultline's unknowns and uncertainties. Instead, the leader and team know what variables affect the organization, where they stand, and what must be done next. They are confident and energized. Interim results themselves have a natural pull effect—they entice teams toward the end goal. But here is the difference: Methodical Innovators do not pause with success. Instead, they use the results and analysis to set the agenda for the next iteration.

Methodical Innovators make wide use of the results. They communicate effectively to all stakeholders and their own teams, thereby building credibility. They analyze individual and team performance and share feedback. Finally, they lean on the results and data analysis to set the agenda for the next iteration.

The CCACC framework is a simple way to capture of the methods used by Digital Champions. Whether they use a written framework or not, they have a clear process to digital transformations. They continuously apply the 10 Rules and perfect the use of data-driven analysis, decision-making, and action. As a result, Methodical Innovators are always personally transforming ahead of the business. Their confidence grows as they succeed.

Confronting, Comprehending, Accepting, Committing, and Continuing is not just for leaders at the top. The effect of the analyses and calls to action is such that the framework extends well into their teams. The leader's management process impacts the style of leaders in the team as well. All this leads to better alignment, more capacity, and clear decision-making. Superior results follow.

> Confronting, Comprehending, Accepting, Committing, and Continuing is not just for leaders at the top.

How Methodical Innovators Apply the 10 Rules

In the process of confronting, comprehending, and accepting the change, Methodical Innovators practice three critical rules: prioritizing customers over competitors, replacing assumptions with data, and learning about digital technologies. When they commit to act and sustain that commitment, they begin to practice all the 10 Rules. To be clear, they do not begin by thinking about everything comprehensively, as we have discussed here. What is described in this persona and the 10 Rules is not documented as a rulebook. Data analysis reveals that their method gets perfected and ingrained through experimentation, monitoring results to see what is working, iterative improvements, and continuous adherence.

In Part IV, I present a playbook that shows how you Methodical Innovators practice certain rules as day-to-day habits and how they apply other rules regularly in iterative cycles of execution. The idea is to transition our discussion from theory into practice and, in the process, help everyone to become Methodical Innovators.

Why Everyone Has a Chance

I said earlier that Digital Age leaders are not born but made. Not everyone is born with the outsized personality of political leaders such as Gandhi, Dr. King, JFK, Helmut Kohl, or Margaret Thatcher. Nor can everyone be Jack Welch, Bill Gates, Steve Jobs, Sergio Marchionne, or Carlos Ghosn.

> To be clear, they do not begin by thinking about everything comprehensively, as we have discussed here. What is described in this persona and the 10 Rules is not documented as a rulebook. Data analysis reveals that their method gets perfected and ingrained through experimentation, monitoring results to see what is working, iterative improvements, and continuous adherence.

The concept of a "naturally gifted" leader does not apply to digital transformations. In Part I of the book, we defined the Digital Faultline and learned that when we understand the forces behind that faultline, we will know how to deal with them. In Part II, we saw the 10 Rules of highly successful organizations and their leaders. And now we have discussed an abstracted Methodical Innovator's persona and the technique it follows. Clearly, this technique develops after understanding the situation, developing a game plan, and executing toward that plan for a while. In other words, the process followed by the Methodical Innovator persona are acquired over time. They are refined and perfected with practice. They are reinforced by success and efficiency derived from the process. That is why I say that leaders will be made—through their own efforts.

Methodical Innovators are not larger-than-life, naturally gifted, and versatile leaders. They painstakingly understand and learn everything there is to about transformations. They tailor and practice the 10 Rules until they master them. And they never stop adapting and changing. This is how leaders in the Digital Age are made—not born. Anyone with the will to succeed and the tenacity to lay a foundation and adopt this persona can become a Methodical Innovator.

PART IV

APPLYING THE 10 RULES: THE METHODICAL INNOVATOR'S PLAYBOOK

CHAPTER 1

INTRODUCTION TO THE METHODICAL INNOVATOR'S PLAYBOOK

The endeavor of *Crossing the Digital Faultline* is to provide readers with a framework to understand the change at a macro level and develop a framework for personal, team, and organizational change. It is now time to put to use what we have learned. But first, let us check our compasses to see where we have come thus far in this journey.

In Part I—We reviewed the Digital Age and the forces beneath the Digital Faultline that make it constantly shifting ground. We have a better understanding of how companies evolve to become digitally converged enterprises. Now we also know why getting away from the faultline is the first critical milestone.

In Part II—We learned about the 10 Rules leaders that Methodical Innovators master to transform their own style, their teams, and eventually their organizations. We also learned that the 10 Rules are connected and how their constant use creates a snowball effect. At the core is the constant use of data to understand situations, develop strategies, act, and measure progress.

In Part III—We reviewed the persona of Methodical Innovators. No one is a born digital-transformation leader; this persona, like any other, is a set of acquired skills and styles. We explored in detail their process of Confronting, Comprehending, Accepting, Committing, and Continuing or sustaining action (CCACC). Data tells us that their first objective is not to transform overnight. It is to get a point of control—in other words, to cross the faultline. We learned that their mastery of the 10 Rules develops over time and that everyone can practice and elevate to become a Methodical Innovator. Everyone has a chance to learn, tailor, and apply the Methodical Innovator persona and the 10 Rules in their transformations.

In Part IV—We develop a step-by-step action plan aimed at transforming your personal style as a leader by using the Methodical Innovator's Playbook. This is essentially an abstraction of the process followed by successful leaders, and it is designed help you get rolling with the application of the 10 Rules. We will see how the rules are applied from strategy to planning and implementation until it is clear how the faultline is crossed.

In the process you will see the remaining two stages of the CCACC framework—Commit and Continue—come to life. The Methodical Innovator's Playbook is designed to get you and your team galvanized into a new way of doing things with simple real-world activities.

In this playbook, I take you back to the days when you first learned to ride a bike, giving guidelines and encouragement. Things may sound theoretical, and the only way to make it real is by undertaking the various activities outlined. Remember, it is only when you start pedaling, balancing, and pedaling that you can stay upright and advance!

The Methodical Innovator's Playbook (MIP)

Successful leaders arrive at a repeatable formula for achieving consistent results only after several attempts. What we will do now is extrapolate and apply the 10 Rules so that you can adopt the right process from the get-go. The Methodical Innovator's Playbook (MIP) is a template that you can tailor to your specific situation and is laid out in four easy steps. Each step has key concepts followed by steps for you and your team to practice or personalize (Figure 27).

FIGURE 27. PLAYBOOK FOR PERSONAL TRANSFORMATION

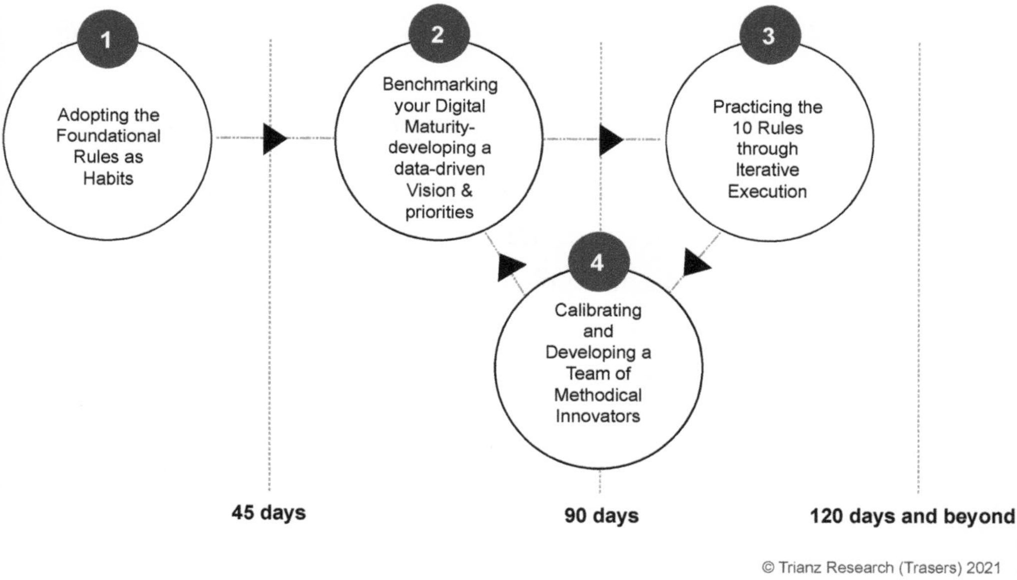

© Trianz Research (Trasers) 2021

Step 1: Adopting Certain Foundational Rules as Habits

Not all rules have the same role in the transformation process. Successful leaders follow some of the 10 Rules, which I call the foundational rules, as everyday habits. This is a transition to a fact-based, depersonalized outcome. This shift is a critical first step in the journey—the more you adopt the foundational rules as habits, the easier it becomes to utilize all of the rules.

Step 2: Benchmarking Your Digital Maturity and Developing a Data-Driven Vision and Priorities

Here, the rubber of personal change meets the road to transformation. It will require you to review data and benchmark your company or organization against the best in class (team, role, etc.). You will understand how to identify gaps and how to fill them. You will arrive at the right priorities and decisions and clearly communicate the steps toward change. All of this will be accomplished by using data without emotional judgment or attachment.

Step 3: Practicing the 10 Rules through Iterative Execution

As you adopt the habits, analyze your situation, and communicate your vision, you will launch the transformation of your group. When you and your team begin implementing priorities, the remaining rules—which I call the derivative rules—come into play. When each iterative cycle of transformation is executed, the team begins to perfect the habits and application of the 10 Rules. This results in a more objective evaluation of outcomes and superior decision-making. As its leader, you would have begun leading the organization across the Digital Faultline.

Step 4: Calibrating and Developing a Team of Methodical Innovators

Methodical Innovators value their teams immensely and provide everyone an opportunity to succeed. Their teams also go through the process of confronting, comprehending, accepting, and committing to change in Steps 1 and 2. However, it is the analysis of current maturity and developing a new digital vision that accelerates their learning. Change is still hard, and the reality is that some will "get it" while others will not. Not all those who get it will be brave enough to implement what you have asked of them. Calibrating and aligning your team is vital because a leader cannot execute successfully without the right team.

In this time of great uncertainty and stress, the last thing a leader should do is to impose an additional mental burden on the minds of team members. The art and science is to put everyone through a 120-day or four-month action plan outlined in this MIP. Less talk and more action is the way forward.

In developing the vision and priorities, you will work with your team on the new approach. As you execute new initiatives with the new style, change will begin to take root automatically and not by way of imposition from on high. Results will become clear, team confidence will improve, and they will begin to enjoy this new data- and rules-based method of transformation.

Always remember that crossing the Digital Faultline is not an individual but a team endeavor. The goal of the Playbook is to not just to help you transform personally but to help create a team of Methodical Innovators, thus scaling your team's capacity and speed of decision-making.

> Always remember that crossing the Digital Faultline is not an individual but a team endeavor.

ADOPTING THE HABITS OF METHODICAL INNOVATORS

What makes Rafael Nadal, Serena Williams, Kobe Bryant, Michael Jordan, Magic Johnson, Lebron James, Maradona, Pele, or Mia Hamm the greatest stars of tennis, basketball, or soccer? Why are Viv Richards, Sachin Tendulkar, Shane Warne, or Wasim Akram remembered for their cricket prowess long after they retired? The extraordinary success of all athletes can be traced to four main elements: great talent, an unparalleled desire to compete and win, learning the right technique, and endless practice.

There are many who are born with great talent, but their success is short-lived. What sets apart athletes who deliver a lifetime of performance is technique and practice—well after they have become champions.

FIGURE 28. METHODICAL INNOVATOR'S PLAYBOOK

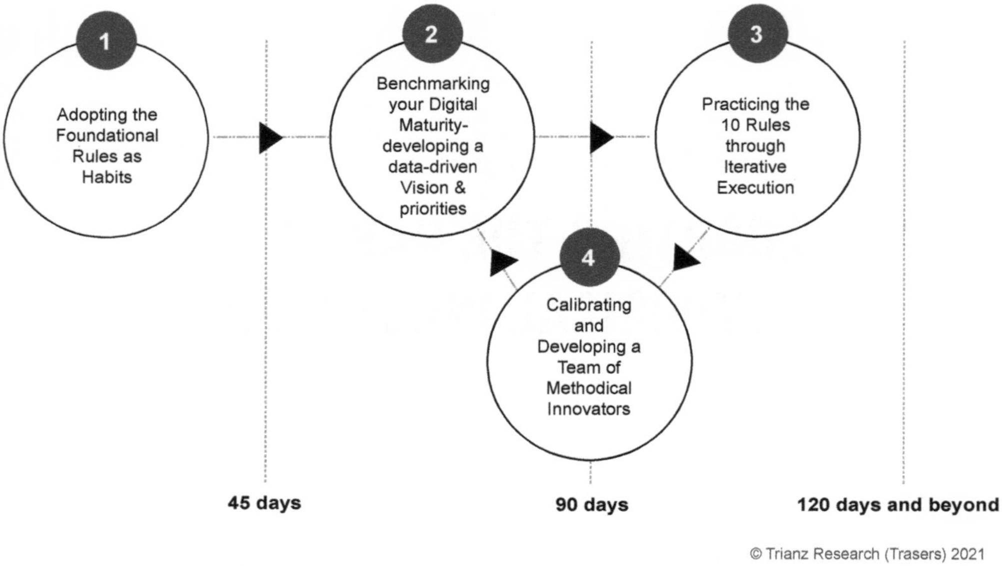

1 Adopting the Foundational Rules as Habits

2 Benchmarking your Digital Maturity-developing a data-driven Vision & priorities

3 Practicing the 10 Rules through Iterative Execution

4 Calibrating and Developing a Team of Methodical Innovators

45 days   **90 days**   **120 days and beyond**

© Trianz Research (Trasers) 2021

Fundamental Rules

The foundational skills in basketball are shooting, dribbling, screening, passing, footwork, and finishing. Dribbling, dunking, defense, and rebounding are advanced skills built on the fundamentals. Leadership and decision-making in the context of digitalization is also similarly governed by rules, as we have seen. Methodical Innovators adopt some of these as fundamental rules or daily habits. These drive every aspect of their work ethic and management process. There are yet other rules that are applied as required during various phases of iterative strategy and execution cycles—the derivative rules of methodical leadership.

Figure 29 shows you the foundational rules on top and the derivative rules placed in an iterative cycle. Learning about customers, industry technologies, value propositions, outcomes, and managing expectations is fundamental. Looking at challenges, opportunities, and even behaviors through a data-driven lens is vital. Once you begin executing iteratively, that the remaining rules come into play. These are applied in conjunction with the basic habits you develop as a leader.

FIGURE 29. FOUNDATIONAL AND DERIVATIVE RULES

Foundational Rules Practiced as Habits

- **Rule #1:** Prioritize Customer-Centricity over Competitive Differentiation
- **Rule #2:** Replace Assumptions with Data Analysis
- **Rule #6:** Learn to Use Digital Technology to Be an Effective Business Leader
- **Rule #8:** Technology Does Not Make Transformations Effective—People Do!
- **Rule #10:** Be Aggressive but Set Realistic Expectations

Derivative Rules Applied during Iterative Execution

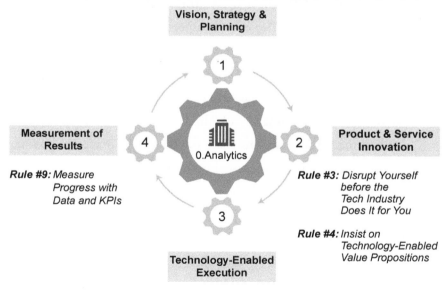

Vision, Strategy & Planning

Measurement of Results

Product & Service Innovation

Rule #9: Measure Progress with Data and KPIs

Rule #3: Disrupt Yourself before the Tech Industry Does It for You

Rule #4: Insist on Technology-Enabled Value Propositions

Technology-Enabled Execution

Rule #5: Break Functional Silos to Become an Experience-Driven Organization

Rule #7: Strategize and Execute in Quick Iterations

© Trianz Research (Trasers) 2021

249

Developing Habits of Success—The Foundational Rules of Digital Leadership

The great Kobe Bryant's basketball work ethic is legendary.

Kobe's basketball practices would begin a few hours before the rest of his teammates showed up and would continue after they came in. In one practice session, Kobe did not leave the court until he had scored eight hundred baskets. In another, he practiced one single shot for an entire hour—shooting from the same midrange spot. Finally, there was an instance when his right arm was in a plaster cast due to injury, so he practiced shooting with his left hand. This dedication to practice continued after he had won three NBA championships, an MVP award, and an Olympic gold medal.

Similarly, the Methodical Innovator's techniques and skills are honed through practice. The effortless performance that customers, investors, peers, teams, and partners see is due to behind-the-curtain practice. The better the performance of an organization, the harder its leaders have practiced their version of the 10 Rules. No one illustrated this point better than Muhammad Ali.

Muhammad Ali, "The Greatest," stayed fit and practiced boxing in the gym harder than anyone else. Legend has it that Arnold Schwarzenegger once visited Ali while he was working out. Schwarzenegger saw Ali doing sit-ups, and when the long session ended, he asked Ali whether he was overdoing it and if it hurt. Ali's response was, "I don't start counting my sit-ups till it pains. There is no gain without the pain."

He went on to say, "Every day of exercise and practice in the gym was painful. But I knew I wanted to spend the rest of my life as a winner and a champion."

Five of the 10 Rules are foundational, and nothing goes right without mastering and applying these rules regularly. The deeper your understanding of these foundational rules, the more consistently you will put them into practice. The more you measure progress, the stronger the connection you will make with the fundamental drivers of change. The more data-driven and timely your decision-making is, the higher your probability of success. The better the results, the more sustained the organizational commitment.

Table 7 shows the specific actions behind the foundational rules that Methodical Innovators continuously take.

Five of the 10 Rules are foundational, and nothing goes right without mastering and applying these rules regularly.

TABLE 7. FOUNDATIONAL RULES PRACTICED AS HABITS

RULE	DESCRIPTION
Rule #1: Prioritize Customer Centricity over Competitive Differentiation	Prioritizing everything around customers, employees, or partners is paramount. Everything else, especially your competition, is secondary unless that competition has proven to be better than you in digitalizing their business.
Rule #2: Replace Assumptions with Data Analysis	Every significant conclusion or decision must be based on facts, data, and insights. Objective, data-driven insights on vision, priorities, strategies, and structures come first—prior experience is overlaid to make the most sense of data.
Rule #6 Learn How to Use Digital Technologies to Be an Effective Business Leader	Technology is going to be pervasive in all aspects of business. The accountability for making IT perform will be with business executives, and technology skills will thus become essential. Develop a step-by-step plan for your role with the help of your own IT—ask them about what you need to learn, and they will help.
Rule #8: Technology Does Not Make Digital Transformations Effective—People Do! Invest in Your Talent	Invest in formal training for your own leaders and extended teams. The cost of training forms less than 5 percent of your budget but is the number one driver of success.
Rule #10: Be Aggressive but Set Realistic Stakeholder Expectations	Realistically assess execution timelines; do not be too aggressive. Set expectations with all stakeholders that transformation takes time while underlining the need to move fast. A leader's credibility before results speak is entirely their word.

SPECIFIC PRACTICE ACTIONS

- Invest in deeply understanding what your customers, suppliers, partners, and influencers care about.
- Draw on internal resources and engage with research firms—constantly study data and trends. Always center your initiatives around customers.

- Partner with IT to deploy a strong foundation of data, insights, and analytics. In the interim, your team and IT should deliver data-driven insights on customers, partners, suppliers, employees, products, and so on through the swiftest means possible.
- Always structure your business meetings and reviews to understand insights and make decisions based on what data tell you.

- Build self-awareness of the fundamental technology pillars of transformation: cloud, analytics, digital, IoT, and cybersecurity.
- Understand enough to be effective in your role: the role of technologies, the right platforms for your industry, implementation cycles, monitoring progress, and required talent. Create technology-learning forums for your teams.
- Always collaborate closely with CIO/IT to develop joint decision-making processes through transformation cycles.
- Always ask how technology can be incorporated to capture an opportunity or solve a challenge right from the beginning.

- Decouple training from strategy and execution. Map individual roles from the top down, identifying required training before, during, and after an initiative.
- Always assess and have talent certified for you to know what they have learned and for them to gain confidence.

- Plan carefully and factor in risks and contingencies. Because the faultline is full of unknowns, stick to conservative timelines, especially in the initial cycles.
- Always monitor risks closely throughout the cycle and adjust or adapt as needed. Communicate progress rhythmically with all stakeholders.

Playbook Step 1: Setting the Rules in Motion

Table 8 outlines the five most important questions that you and your team need to get answers for before beginning a transformation process. These questions must be tailored to your industry, business, function, your role and area(s) of responsibility, and team(s). To clarify, stakeholders for a leader in marketing would be entirely different from those for a leader in human capital or procurement.

TABLE 8. STEPS OF THE METHODICAL INNOVATOR'S PLAYBOOK

Playbook Step 1:

	CONFRONT	COMPREHEND	ACCEPT
Key Questions on Change Due to Digitalization	• What is the change taking place among customers in my industry? The important topics to focus on—how customers define value today, their budgets and spending priorities, their expectations from companies in your industry, and their buying process.		
	• How do these changes affect my company and my role?		
	• What new value propositions, products, services, business models, or processes are coming up in my business or technology function?		
	• Who are my main stakeholders (based on role), and how are the expectations of my stakeholders (customers, employees, partners, top management peers) affected?		
	• How are my employees being affected at work, and what do they need to learn to be successful?		
	• How does the digital maturity of my function compare with my competitors? Focus on process digitalization, experiences, use of analytics and modern technologies.		
Required Resources for Analysis	• What company data should I explore to answer these questions?		
	• What external data should I collect to benchmark against my competitors?		
	• Who in my direct team and my IT team can help answer these questions? (Avoid consultants and assign specific responsibilities to your team members.)		
The Data Collection and Analysis Process	• Write down quick answers to the questions as you feel appropriate (i.e., without referring to any external data or insights). Ask your team to do so as well.		
	• Collect data for each question and generate insights that help answer each question separately and systematically.		
	• Benchmark your digital maturity by utilizing an external data collection agency.		
	• Compare the quick answers you wrote down with data-driven insights to see the difference data makes.		
Expected Results— Team Alignment and Shared Understanding	• Recognition of the change among customers and other stakeholders, technology-led value propositions, impact of all this on your role.		
	• Relative positioning/progress versus competitors and best in class in your role.		
	• The importance and sources of data related to your function and role.		
	• How your team and employees are affected by the change, what their expectations are, what they need to change, and what specific skills they need to learn.		

Cumulative time: → 30 Days

To succeed in Step 1 of the MIP, it is critical that each question be tailored and adapted as necessary. It is also important that answers to these questions are as data-driven as possible. This exercise must be executed as a short five- to nine-week internal project by assigning specific tasks to your team members. You must personally monitor their progress every week.

Clearly, Step 1 is about much more than getting answers to the list of questions you have developed. It automatically puts you into motion with the first foundational rules.

- By asking tailored questions around customer behavior, you practice customer centricity.

- By collecting data, you are replacing assumptions.

- By learning about technology's role in your function, you will partner better with IT.

- By studying the human dimension, you are preparing to invest in your people and so on.

Engaging Your Team

Step 1 starts changing the way your team thinks about these major transitional issues. In the process of finding answers, you are not just beginning a personal transition to becoming a Methodical Innovator; by involving them, you are making this a team effort. You are signaling the change in approach, priorities, management, and collaboration that is about to come. Here are important ways to engage the team:

1. The development of questions outlined in MIP Step 1 must be done as a group—involve your senior leadership team.

2. Assign the task of collecting data from within the company (in collaboration with IT) to your direct team based on their responsibilities.

3. Ask your direct team to analyze their respective areas and support each of them individually.

4. When reviewing the analysis for your overall organization, be sure to include all your senior team members.

It is absolutely critical that you are deeply involved your team's discussions, framing of challenges, collection of data, and generation of review of insights. You must be personally convinced by the insights—see, feel, and hear them.

Methodical Innovator Persona Self-Assessment: Compare Initial and Data-Driven Answers

At the end of the exercise, compare the answers based on your data-driven insights to your initial gut-instinct answers. Assess your results. You should see results such as:

- Right answers validated: The data-driven answers validate your instinct and experience in some cases and supplement them with data-driven insights. You can now be confident about your initial answers.

- Wrong answers identified and corrected: Some of your initial answers have been proven wrong to varying degrees. The data and insights you gathered during the exercise will show you surprising discoveries and create a consciousness in the team to avoid making incorrect assumptions.

Step 1 gets you and the team aligned on change, its impact, technologies, and the organizational gaps. In Step 2, you will see that it is much easier to align peers and superiors when they are presented with irrefutable data-driven insights and logic.

DEVELOP A DATA-DRIVEN DIGITAL VISION, STRATEGY, AND PRIORITIES

The Digital Champions in this book had several "first-mover" advantages. While framing a vision and priorities, they initially experimented with the little steps. They went on the offensive and set the tone for the encounter as opposed to constantly reacting to competition. Finally, they were driving change in a stable and growing economic environment (2010–2020). They had the luxury of time.

The ground conditions have now changed. Developing a digital vision in the post-COVID era is the most difficult task leaders face as they try to break away from the Digital Faultline. You will first have to understand a subject that is inherently complex, now made more difficult by a volatile revenue picture and limited resources in a recessionary environment. Finally, the windows of opportunity are rapidly shrinking as customers habits change and aggressive competitors race ahead. Figure 30 provides a frame of reference: a series of undisputable facts in the environment in which leaders must operate.

FIGURE 30. METHODICAL INNOVATOR'S PLAYBOOK

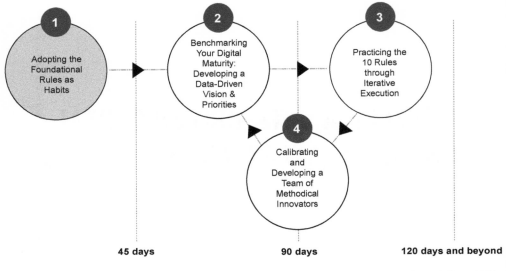

© Trianz Research (Trasers) 2021

To successfully cross the Digital Faultline, you must create a well-prioritized vision and priorities in short timelines. Leaders of companies and business functions in the early stage of transformation face an arduous task. Those who are already driving change have leaped ahead in the game.

Let us discuss ways to develop a relevant and practical vision in this environment.

The Dimensions of a Digital Vision

The single most important audience for your company vision is the customer. As we have discussed, this term applies to external customers and partners as well as to employees. A fundamental rule in the approach of Methodical Innovators is that they build their visions from the outside in. They evaluate a problem or an opportunity from the customer end and work backward into the organization.

There are two important elements to consider in developing a customer-centric vision (Figure 31). These are the value or utility from your products and the life cycle experience from evaluating, buying, and utilizing to renewal. The goal is to quickly move from low to high value (y-axis) and toward endearing experience for the customer (x-axis). The goal is to evolve step by step to arrive at the highest value experience square (upper-right square).

FIGURE 31. VALUE-ORIENTED DIGITAL VISIONS

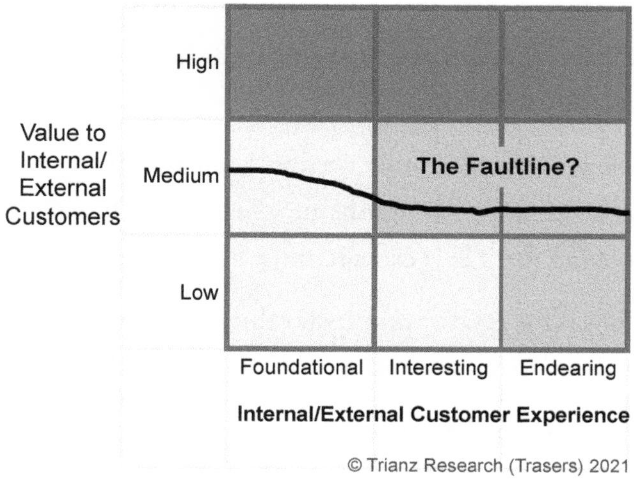

© Trianz Research (Trasers) 2021

However, the process and speed of developing visions for external and internal customers varies. Let us look at both.

Developing Highly Digitalized Products and Services for External Customers

The process of product-service transformation for external customers begins with a series of questions on both the x- and y-axes of Figure 30 The x-axis questions will cover real or perceived needs, priorities, brand association, value perception, pricing, and alternatives. Questions on the y-axis will revolve around brand or product awareness, evaluation, buying experience, and use.

Leaders from marketing, sales, service, and R&D who are involved with product management must first list key questions. For a single product or service, here are some key questions to ask:

- What is the performance trend of the product—is it growing, flat, or declining?

- What is the customer feedback on the product—are they satisfied and what are the new features or functions they are looking for? (This exercise must be done at a detailed level.)

- How is the need or priority for this product category changing? Is the demand increasing, reducing, or staying flat? Why?

- What alternatives are emerging on the horizon for customers? Are there other ways to solve the same problem?

- What technologies are affecting this product or service and how?

- What are my competitors doing? What next-generation propositions are being launched?

- What is the buyer's journey, and what is their experience with this product? (This exercise must be done at a detailed level.)

- What is the customer life cycle, what is their experience, and what is their feedback for improvement? (This exercise must be done at a detailed level.)

- How do we know if what we are doing is going to work (for in-flight transformations)?

- How do we become the leader in the speed of developing products and services?

You might conceive of several more detailed questions related to the product and customers at a segment level. However, it is only when these fundamental questions are fully answered that the efforts put in by your teams really delivers results.

There is an inherent cultural change that companies must go allow: shifting from the traditional "Build it and they will come" mindset to "What do they need and how can we do it the best and fastest?" The hi-tech industry arrives at product or service value definitions and delivers them faster than any other industry (TGTS data).

The hi-tech companies establish value propositions using a problem-solution approach called "design thinking." This essentially turns the culture from inside out to outside in. The second concept is the digitalization and acceleration of the product-development cycle. These are two vital and independent topics that everyone involved in product management must study. I introduce them in brief to demonstrate why hi-tech companies have such a high customer acceptance and the fastest product-development pace.

> There is an inherent cultural change that companies must go allow: shifting from the traditional "Build it and they will come" mindset to "What do they need and how can we do it the best and fastest?"

Concept #1: Design Thinking

Design thinking began as a technique for solving problems in the early 1990s in Silicon Valley. It went mainstream when Stanford University made it part of the engineering curriculum. In bringing a concept, a solution, or value proposition to life using design thinking, six major activities are involved. These are:

Step 1: Empathize with the user.

Step 2: Define the problem as seen by the user.

Step 3: Ideate or explore multiple solutions to the same problem.

Step 4: Prototype the most viable alternatives.

Step 5: Test with actual users to validate problem, solution, value, and experiences.

Step 6: Implement and launch.

Figure 32 shows the cyclical or iterative design thinking process to define and execute on a new product or service.

FIGURE 32. DESIGN-THINKING PROCESS

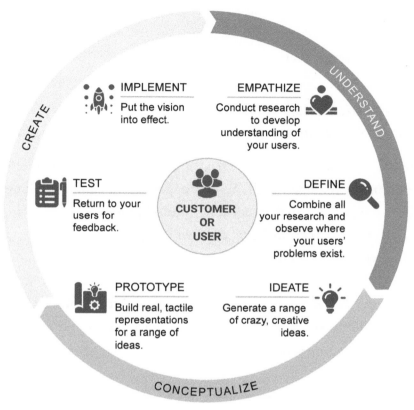

© Trianz Research (Trasers) 2021

With the customer at the center, design thinking underscores the premise that a need or value always originates with the customer, is validated by the customer, and ends with the customer.

The hi-tech industry is the leading user of design thinking. First, it is centered on users (tech-speak for customers), problems are user-defined, alternatives are presented to users, and acceptance testing is done with users. Second, from the very identification of the problem to the results that validate or invalidate a concept, it relies on data and removes bias. In effect, design thinking embodies Rule #1: "Prioritize customer centricity over competitive differentiation." Leaders from R&D, marketing, and sales from companies in traditional industries must learn much more about design thinking. This will help them to develop a customer-centric model for defining value and change internal culture.

Concept #2: Digitalization of the Product-Development Cycle

The hi-tech industry has also excelled in digitalizing the product-development life cycle itself. Several stages of the design-thinking cycle in Figure 32, such as ideating, prototyping, and testing, are now digitalized. They are being done with AI, virtual or augmented reality, virtual prototypes, and digital testing. AR and VR allow hi-tech companies to create multiple digital alternatives for product or services. They also use real-world customers to test virtual products. The net effect is shortened product-development cycles and reduced overall costs. Continuous customer involvement increases the probability of success.

Using TGTS data, we constructed a product/service competitiveness matrix (review Figure 8). This matrix shows how design thinking and digitalization help hi-tech to deliver the highest volume of products with the best customer acceptance levels in the shortest possible cycle times.

The matrix highlights the perils of falling behind in this race across the Digital Faultline. Some 30–40 percent of companies across industries will fade into obscurity or die over the next five to ten years because of their inability to reinvent rapidly enough.

The paradigm shifts in thinking, the scale of effort and business focus required, is such that these changes cannot be accomplished overnight. What leaders of R&D/product development, marketing, and sales must do is collectively prioritize and articulate a well validated, design thinking-based product/service vision. This must be shared first with their company's leadership and then to their teams. As a second step, they should deploy the right technology infrastructure to digitalize and accelerate their R&D cycles.

Methodical Innovator Persona Self-Assessment: Envisioning a Customer-Centric Product/ Service Development

Review recent product launches. Review all of your new product or service launches over the past three years and classify them as a success, failure, or abandoned. For each of these classifications, note the reasons for success, failure, or decision to abort. In addition, spell out customer engagement in each step of the process. In the case of successes, you will note high customer engagement in pilots and feedback-based adaptation. For failures, you will note low customer engagement, lack of clear customer value, or lack of differentiation. Aborted projects might, for example, be caused by cost overruns, lack of customer validation, failure to perform as expected, or market change. The key questions to be asked are: How well did the development teams engage with customers throughout the cycle, and are outcomes influenced by the degree of customer engagement? They should be.

Review product-development cycles. Within each step of your development cycle, note places where virtual design (of multiple options), prototyping, and customer testing occur. Also note the cycle time for each phase and the time it takes to complete the entire development cycle itself.

Finally, plot your position on the x- and y-axes of Figure 31 (Value-oriented digital visions) from earlier in this chapter. Which square are you in? If you are positioned in the lowest row, your first goal is to move up in customer appeal. If you are in the middle row, your goal is to move up again. If you are in the left-hand columns, then your goal is to accelerate development and move to the right. But the first objective is to always move up on the x-axis, i.e., appeal of products and services to customers.

Developing a Services-Oriented Vision for Internal Customers

In Rule #6, "Break functional silos and create connected experiences," we discussed the concept of internal customers. Great end-customer experiences are only possible when processes are integrated and digitalized. Internal functions that consume your services or are part of cross-functional processes such as "quote to cash" or "issue to resolution" or "hire to retire" are those internal customers.

Methodical Innovators take internal customer centricity to the extreme. They are driven by the needs of their customers. Not only does this help them to accurately prioritize, but it also encourages internal customers to become invested in the process. In turn, this results in continuous engagement, feedback, and acceptance when new capabilities are rolled out.

Let us say you have digitalized the HR processes of interviewing, onboarding, and payroll. When employees have to call a 1-800 number to inquire about their insurance coverage, their experience breaks down. But if you treat them as customers, you will offer an online employee portal or app that offers everything these customers might need. However, for HR to enable all this, collaboration with finance and legal is critical.

Thus, in Digital Champion companies, a network effect gets created. Each function begins to force others to change due to interlinked, cross-functional processes. Over time, the entire value chain becomes digitalized, delivering ease of working and high velocity. A connectedness is created across customer acquisition, value delivery, and value enablement. While the internal benefits are obvious, the net result is great experiences for the end customers.

To develop a great internal customer vision, begin by formally asking questions related to your function. Here is an initial list that you might build on:

- Who are my internal customers/stakeholders?

- What services or products do they receive from my organization?

- What value do they place on these services?

- Are my internal customers satisfied or dissatisfied? What are their challenges?

- How are my peers changing their own business models and processes, and how should we change ours in response? What are the points of integration?

- What are my peers' emerging priorities and how should my organization's priorities align?

- How do we prepare these internal customers for what we are launching?

- What ongoing communication mechanisms are required to ensure alignment?

The transformation game for internal operations is all about the design and delivery of highly digitalized, high-velocity/low-touch, consistent, and connected experiences. The key is to identify and continually develop internal customer-driven priorities.

Formally Determining Stakeholder Priorities

Put together a list of subfunctions or services that your function provides to other functions in the company. For example, an HCM leader may provide talent acquisition, goal setting, training and development, performance management and compensation, etc., all of which are utilized by all other business functions in the organization.

> The transformation game for internal operations is all about the design and delivery of highly digitalized, high-velocity/low-touch, consistent, and connected experiences. The key is to identify and continually develop internal customer-driven priorities.

List the other functions in the company that utilize these services and the key stakeholders in these functions.

Prepare a formal set of questions that you would ask of leaders in these functions about their upcoming digitalization needs from your organization. These needs could be in the form of new process capabilities, analytics, experiences, or system level integrations.

Summarize the needs that are common among various functions and list all the needs. Reconfirm these needs with the stakeholders.

Map the needs based on their value to customers and digital-transformation impact in the 3x3 framework provided in the beginning of this chapter.

This forms one of the two sources of priorities and one of the important outcomes an internal customer validation: alignment and buy-in. When you roll out new, improved capabilities, those stakeholders will be your allies.

The name of the game is to define value and experiences in a way that appeals to them, i.e., outside in and not inside out. Next, we look at second piece of this puzzle—using data to help you develop such a vision.

Benchmark-Driven Vision, Strategy Development, and Prioritization

Given that the forces on the Digital Faultline are not actually visible, you do not know what you do not know. Compounding the problem are the internal pulls and pressures and competing priorities and biases. This is where Rule #3, "Replace assumptions with data analysis," helps. The most important things to know are customer value and priorities, technologies, and value propositions, competitively. If you do not know any one of these variables, you could end up focusing on themes that do not matter to customers.

Benchmarking is a process by which a data services company collects data that reveal your digital maturity across dimensions such as customer or stakeholder centricity, value propositions, the digital IQ (awareness/understanding) of your leadership, the degree to which your processes are digitalized, talent readiness, and your decision-making culture on a competitive basis. In effect, benchmarking tells you where you are today, and where your competitors and Digital Champions are (Figure 33).

FIGURE 33. BENCHMARKING AGAINST THE DIGITAL ENTERPRISE EVOLUTION MODEL (DEEM)©

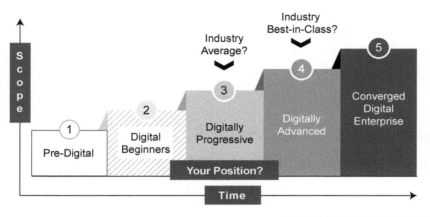

© Trianz Research (Trasers) 2021

Why is it so important to know where you are today? Let me share a lesson I learned from my military academy days that has served me well.

In the final semester of basic training at the military academy, we conducted map-reading exercises. GPS was not yet mass produced, and we did not have access to it. From an elevated ground with panoramic views, we would use a map and compass to identify the surrounding landmarks and plot our own position. Alternately, we would march distances of fifteen to twenty-five miles and report in at various checkpoints using a map and compass or landmarks. We completed this exercise more than a dozen times until we were totally bored with them.

In his closing lecture on the topic, the instructor summed up why we had endured that repetitive exercise. "Whenever you are dropped in a new location and need to get to a target, the first thing you need to know is your own position, not that of the destination. By knowing your own position in relation to the target before you begin, you can objectively explore alternative routes. You will select the one with the highest probability of success—and it may not be the shortest one. By checking your position continuously, you can adjust your route until you get to your destination safely and on time to launch your mission."

Today, knowing exactly where I am and where my team is at time has become second nature in chaotic, turbulent, and difficult times.

The frustrating irony of technology consumption today is this. Everyone uses GPS and Google Maps as a habit when driving to new destinations. But they do not use the same principle of guidance when it comes to launching their digital initiatives.

If formally collected customer needs are the destination, then benchmarking becomes your GPS. It tells you where you are today and what you should prioritize given your current competitive position. If there is one takeaway from this chapter, it is this—you must benchmark and base your vision on the insights from it.

Assessing Your Competitive Digital Maturity and Priorities

Conduct a competitive digital maturity benchmarking exercise to see where your function is in relation to your competition and note best-in-class organizations across various industries. You will require the services of an external organization to collect benchmarking data.

Participate in the benchmarking exercise by providing inputs related to your function.

Generate insights with the help of the benchmarking partner and compare the position of each subfunction or competency in your organization relative to your competitors or Digital Champions.

Develop a second list of priorities based on competitive benchmarking.

Benchmarking will certainly reveal a surprising evaluation of your digital maturity, different than the one you may have believed it to be, and give you an accurate position relative to your competitors and Digital Champions. Such a data-driven evaluation eliminates or minimizes biases and quickly aligns teams, peers, superiors, and even your finance organization.

Crystallizing Your Digital Vision, Strategy, and Priorities

Benchmarking insights must be triangulated with internally assessed needs, data, and dependencies. From this holistic approach emerges a prioritized vision strategy and plan. Here is a step-by-step process to consolidate everything into a digital vision:

- **Triangulation of Benchmarking:** Insights from benchmarking data must be triangulated against inputs from your stakeholders. The gaps revealed by benchmarking will usually correlate closely with the internal inputs. Several logical and credible priorities emerge from this triangulation exercise. Low-hanging fruit or quick wins will also become clearer.

- **Digital Vision and Strategic Objectives:** An important outcome of a data-driven approach is clarity about objectives and priorities. These then help to frame clear and crisp vision statements. Methodical Innovators frame their vision in one to three years as opposed five years. Given the unknowns in the business paradigm today, such a lengthy horizon is just not credible. A vision should outline the purpose of digitalization in terms of competitive value propositions and outcomes. It should outline operating model changes, business outcomes, experiences, and organizational values. Importantly, it must avoid a sole focus on technology. Remember—framing transformations as technology initiatives is one of the top three reasons for failure to cross the Digital Faultline.

- **Execution Priorities and Road Map:** From the vision emerge the specific initiatives for the immediate phase. Initiatives must be framed crisply and expected outcomes defined with proper KPIs. Each of these should be executed using iterative models in no longer than six months to a year at most. Finally, leaders must plan for the required people, consultants, technology, or financial resources. A roadmap outlines the sequence in which such initiatives should be executed.

Strategies from data-driven insights tend to create a "popcorn effect." One idea will trigger another, and you begin to visualize your business differently. Your team is excited with the clarity and wants to race into execution. But there is one important task to take care of: validation.

Validating Your Vision and Setting Expectations

An often overlooked but critical is the validation of your vision, road map, and expectations. In the traditional model, each function builds its own plans, thus perpetuating disconnects. Such disconnects and silos are the enemy of digital enterprise.

Methodical Innovators understand the interconnected nature of their efforts. They test, articulate, and defend their vision repeatedly to ensure alignment with superiors, peers, and their own teams. They host workshops, hold informal discussions with key stakeholders, and work to build a strong coalition for the journey. Conversely, they provide support to peers for their own journeys.

Thus, Methodical Innovators create solid alignment before they present their plans to their superiors. They are also careful in warning about risks and outlining proper mitigation plans. This is how they set realistic expectations and practice foundational Rule #10.

Step 2 of the Methodical Innovator's Playbook is a critical and comprehensive step where you begin to act and move from theory to practice. Given that the activities being described here are not theoretical or restricted to your individual transformation, the output of Step 2 is what your organization should be doing.

The more serious, thorough, and rigorous your execution of Step 2 of the Playbook is, the faster and better you can address a personal and team or organizational transformation, as well as the portfolio of products or services to be delivered to internal or external customers.

Summary: Reimagining Products and Services for External Customers

If you are in R&D/product management, marketing or sales, interview a select set of external customers and partners to understand how they perceive value from your products and services, and how their priorities, choices, and their buying habits are changing.

- Engage an external benchmarking agency to study changing customer needs, definition of value, priorities, and buying journeys.

- Engage an external agency to assess your product-development processes against key competitors to identify gaps in fact-based terms and opportunities to accelerate.

- Develop a products and services vision that addresses the gaps beginning emphasizing foundational needs first and outlining clear, measurable outcomes.

Reimagining Internal Services and Operations

If you are in any internal operational role, formally interview and collect the needs and expectations of your peer functions from your group.

- Engage an external source to assess the digital maturity of your operating value chain against key competitors and present data-driven insights.

- Triangulate external benchmarking insights and identified gaps with internally expressed needs to identify multiple waves of priorities with clear, measurable outcomes.

- Develop an execution plan that covers the priorities, the sequence, dependencies, and governance models for your initiatives.

Engaging Your Team

Assign tasks to each of your direct reports to collect needs from adjacent functions.

- Organize customer behavior and digital maturity benchmarking studies into projects and have key members from your team lead the efforts.

- Involve your senior team in all strategy development exercises.

- Have each of your leaders validate their components of the vision and plan with their counterparts.

PRACTICING THE 10 RULES DURING EXECUTION CYCLES

Let us for a moment imagine what you will have covered in the real world by completing the first two steps in the Methodical Innovator's Playbook.

FIGURE 34. METHODICAL INNOVATOR'S PLAYBOOK

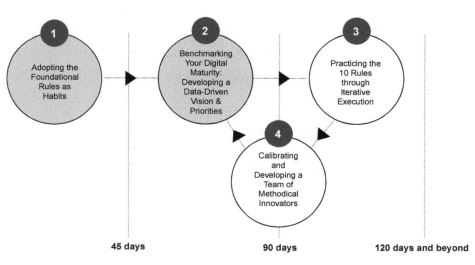

© Trianz Research (Trasers) 2021

With Step 1, you will have begun practicing the foundational rules and understood the impact of change to your industry, company, and role.

In Step 2, you will have engaged with external or internal customers to better understand their needs and priorities. You will also have undertaken a digital maturity benchmarking exercise. You have a good understanding of the gap between their expectations and the value and experiences you are delivering. You will also know the gap between you and your competitors. In other words, you can see whether you are ahead or behind competitors in understanding changing external or internal stakeholder needs. This is *the* most powerful reason and takeaway from competitive benchmarking.

Armed with this understanding, you developed a digital vision for he future. You also mapped out the short- and long-term priorities and have built a well-sequenced plan that will be executed iteratively.

This is a team effort, and so you involve your team in all activities. It is a smart approach for three fundamental reasons. One, your team begins to learn the fundamentals along with you and a natural alignment occurs. Second, their participation results in vesting, and they are automatically bought into your new approach. And finally, when it is time to implement the vision, there is little explanation required—they are ready to execute the vision as a team.

Graduating from Practicing Foundational to Derivative Rules

In the beginning of the playbook, we discussed the concept of a system in which the 10 Rules work. In that, we reviewed the foundational rules that Methodical Innovators practice as habits and the derivative rules applied during iterative execution.

In Step 1, you understood what the digital-transformation challenge is all about and how it affects your organization. In Step 2, you collected internal and external data to develop your vision, priorities, and execution plans. All along, you have been practicing the foundational rules of the game of transformation (Table 9):

TABLE 9. FOUNDATIONAL RULES APPLIED IN STEPS 1 AND 2

STEPS	MAJOR TASKS	RULES BEING PRACTICED
Step 1: Adopting the Habits of Methodical Innovators	Understanding the meaning of digital transformation and its impact to your industry, company, and your role	Rule #1: Prioritize Customer Centricity Rule #2: Replace Assumptions with Data
Step 2: Develop a Data-Driven Vision and Strategy	Understanding internal needs and priorities	Rule #1: Prioritize Customer Centricity
	Customer Research	Rules #1 and 2
	Competitive Benchmarking	Rule #2: Replace Assumptions with Data
	Vision and Strategy Development	Rule #3: Learn about Digital Technologies
	Iterative Execution Plan and Roadmap	Rule #10: Be Aggressive but Set Realistic Expectations

When you involve your team in the major tasks as explained in Steps 1 and 2, you automatically practice Rule #8, "Technology does not enable digital transformations—people do." The data collection and analysis tasks you assign and the discussions make it essential to learn more about transformations. They begin to practice these rules alongside you, negating the need to explain or impose this new way of working on them.

Let us now see how the derivative rules come into play as you begin transforming. This is best illustrated through the life cycle of a transformational innovative. Several near-term priorities can be grouped to form a transformational initiative, iterative in nature as opposed to the traditional linear and long-execution models.

Figure 33 illustrates the iterative cycle of execution discussed at length previously. Let us see how the derivative rules now come into play.

Vision, Strategy, and Planning

The very fact that your initiative is iterative means that you are employing Rule #7, "Strategize and execute in quick iterations."

Product and Service Innovation

In this phase, you are conceptualizing a new product or service either for external or internal customers. Now you focus on delivering the highest value from a customer's point of view, that is the greatest experience, a high ROTI, and a "cool product." In effect, you will use Rule #3, "Disrupt yourself before the tech industry does it for you," and Rule #4, "Insist on technology-enabled value propositions."

Technology-Enabled Execution

Your teams need to learn new techniques like Agile engineering. This is how Rule #7, "Strategize and execute in quick iterations" comes into play. Depending on the size and scope of your initiative, teams will collaborate and communicate with other functions. This is when Rule #5, "Break functional silos to become an experience-driven organization," should take effect.

Measurement of Results

Right in the beginning of the initiative, you would have determined the measurement of progress and final outcomes. In doing so, you are practicing Rule #9, "Measure progress with data and KPIs."

FIGURE 35. DERIVATIVE RULES APPLIED DURING ITERATIVE EXECUTION

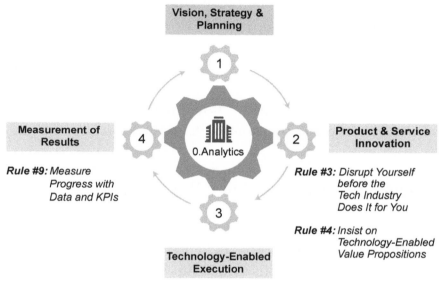

© Trianz Research (Trasers) 2021

As you can see, each of the 10 Rules we have discussed are new but logical ways of doing things. They also ensure great outcomes. Methodical Innovators measure progress on a regular basis and correct course wherever necessary. But as you reach the final stage of an initiative and begin measuring outcomes, the real impact of all 10 Rules comes into play. When results are measured using data, you will have exceeded or met or fallen short of expectations. Whether the outcomes or positive or not, your directional alignment keeps improving with iterations. If the outcomes are positive, you know the team is headed in the right direction. If they are not, then the team is forced to confront and address them. Therefore, any of these outcomes will help you to determine the next set of objectives, outcomes, and execution cycle.

Practicing the Derivative Rules of Methodical Innovators

Over time, these 10 Rules become habits and the way of doing things for Methodical Innovators. Now we will discuss each step of an iterative cycle and the specific actions you must take to apply the derivative rules of successful leaders (Table 10).

Reviewing Progress Using the 10 Rules

Methodical Innovators structure programs tightly. They set team and individual goals, schedule rhythmic business reviews, and use leading indicators (leading KPIs). These KPIs show the likelihood of a certain milestone or goal being achieved. Lagging indicators to show real outcomes and what corrections need to be made.

Depending on the complexity or the number of initiatives being executed, leaders also deploy a transformational program office, which acts as a governance body, monitoring leading indicators, anticipating issues, and tackling them through timely decision-making. Reviews are held at a predetermined time to measure both outcomes and directional alignment. These reviews form the "spine" of practice for Methodical Innovators.

Finally, Methodical Innovators do not follow the concept of "start and finish." Instead, they cross the Digital Faultline as soon as possible, regain control, and sustain the processes of change. The insights from KPI-based measurements define the agenda and priorities for the next iteration of digital transformation.

There is no finish line for winners in digital transformations, as they evolve continuously from one level of maturity to another until they regain full control. They then reset the compass and move toward digital leadership.

TABLE 10. DERIVATIVE RULES OF METHODICAL INNOVATORS

STAGE OF THE ITERATIVE CYCLE	RULE
2. Product/service process innovation	Rule #3: Disrupt yourself before the tech industry does it for you.
	Rule #4: Insist on technology-enabled value propositions.
3. Technology implementation	Rule #7: Strategize and execute in quick iterations.
	Rule #5: Break functional silos to become an experience-driven organization. (Ensure "end to end" stakeholder experiences.)
4. Rollout and measurement	Rule #9: Measure progress with data and KPIs. Be relentless—even after crossing the Digital Faultline.

SPECIFIC PRACTICE ACTIONS

- Focus on the customer and be aggressive to close the expectation gap.
- Use benchmarking data already collected or go into the next level of detail to ensure that your new vision and priorities place you ahead of competition. If there are constraints, get through the first cycle as quickly as possible to break them.

- Create a mapping of customer expectations to your product/service to track the iterations in which they will all be addressed or innovated upon using technology.
- Establish a joint business/IT leadership team to see how the new value proposition can incorporate digital technologies (analytics, cloud, process digitalization, user experience and security).
- If your team lacks the specific skills required to visualize and embed technology, then the services of specialist firms must be used.

- While the vision can be big and ambitious, it should not be complicated and difficult to achieve.
- Make sure that each iteration is tailored to achieve a well-defined set of objectives that form a minimum viable product for the stakeholders. These outcomes should be measurable in KPIs.

- Based on the external products and services sold to your customers or new services delivered internally, deploy a user experience team or organization.
- Its role must be to map, design, and deliver consistent end-to-end experiences to your stakeholders in coordination with relevant functions in the enterprise (another reason to collaborate closely with peers in your initiatives and theirs).

- Using KPIs, determine what specifically defines your point of digital convergence—the point where you cross the Digital Faultline.
- Concentrate resources and efforts to cross the Faultline, and deploy company or function-specific leading and lagging digital KPIs to track business outcomes.
- Analyze results from the first iteration to set the priorities and agenda for improvements, adjustments, or brand-new targets.

© Trianz 2020

Methodical Innovator Playbook: Step 3—Practicing the Rules through Execution Cycles

Step 3 begins once a strategic vision and priorities have been established (Step 2). The team is automatically engaged by the time you have transitioned into execution.

Group one or more related priorities into a transformational initiative. Groupings can be by a subfunction or by a series of interrelated challenges or opportunities.

> There is no finish line for winners in digital transformations, as they evolve continuously from one level of maturity to another until they regain full control. They then reset the compass and move toward digital leadership.

Organize teams that will develop detailed execution plans for each initiative, comprising targeted outcomes, resources, timelines, and measurable business outcomes.

Define a review model for the initiative comprising of leading and lagging KPIs and the frequency of such reviews.

Ensure that the vision being developed under each initiative is aggressive and overcomes a challenge or captures an opportunity, fully leveraging technology.

Implement the initiatives in short bursts using modern techniques such as "Agile" to achieve intermediate goals.

Conduct reviews regularly and rhythmically and measure results through predetermined, lagging KPIs.

Once the goals of a particular iteration are achieved, use the results and learning to refine or establish transformational goals for the next execution cycle.

STEP 4

DEVELOP A TEAM OF METHODICAL INNOVATORS

Selecting the Right Team

Given the complexity of the challenge, it is not possible to across the Digital Faultline without the right team. Therefore, the question is inescapable: do I have the right team?

Leaders can adopt one of two distinct styles to answer this question and assemble the right team.

In one, the leader achieves a certain "nirvana" or enlightenment and assesses the ability of team members to lead effectively. Where needed, the leader makes rapid changes even before the transformation process begins. This approach works when the task is crystallized, there is an approval to hire, and highly talented resources are easily available in the market.

In the second style, the leader achieves "nirvana" but carries the team along, even if they are not yet adept to respond to upcoming needs. The idea is that they, too, learn and understand what leadership in digital transitions is all about.

As you can now see, I have advocated the second style throughout this Methodical Innovator's Playbook. My reasons for doing so are as follows.

First, it will not be easy to hire new talent due to various hiring freezes and financial constraints in this COVID-driven situation. Second, talent that is highly experienced in transformations is not readily available in the market. Third, institutionalized knowledge is easy to lose but is hard to build. Finally, there is a sense of fairness and duty toward existing teams. It has been my experience that, given equal opportunity and clear motivation, a vast majority of team members will rise to the challenge and help you to find success in their new roles. In this latest COVID-driven onslaught of digitalization, the urgency to transform is clear, and there is a natural eagerness to succeed. It is important give everyone an opportunity and take those who can transform with you. Those who do not yet measure up can be coached—and replaced if they do not rise to the task.

This is a moment of truth for most leaders, and it is one I have faced myself. Years of knowledge, shared experiences, loyalties, and associated emotions will undoubtedly surface as you evaluate your teams. Such emotions make it difficult to set aside your feelings and evaluate capabilities objectively. Will all your team members make the digital leadership transition? No, they will not. But most will.

> Years of knowledge, shared experiences, loyalties, and associated emotions will undoubtedly surface as you evaluate your teams. Such emotions make it difficult to set aside your feelings and evaluate capabilities objectively. Will all your team members make the digital leadership transition? No, they will not. But most will.

It is important to establish a shared and well understood leadership model and style for transformation. The key is to create a formal framework for each leader to transition to becoming Methodical Innovators in their individual roles.

FIGURE 36. METHODICAL INNOVATOR'S PLAYBOOK

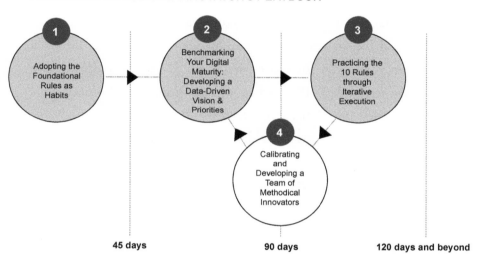

© Trianz Research (Trasers) 2021

Your Team Begins to Change with Steps 1 and 2 of the Playbook

By engaging your team Steps 1 and 2 of the playbook, you have already triggered a change in them. Let us quickly recap their involvement and experiences in these two steps:

Step 1—Adopting the Foundational Habits. The team has contributed to framing the right questions on industry change and its effect on your business. They have also seen a not-so-subtle change in your leadership style. A newfound focus, an insistence on data, and a step-by-step approach toward finding the right answers forces them to respond.

289

Step 2—Develop a Data-Driven Digital Vision, Strategy, and Priorities. The team have contributed to creating the custom benchmarking questionnaires. They have engaged with associated functions to identify what they need from your organization. They have analyzed benchmarking results and helped develop your vision and priorities.

In effect, your team has begun practicing the 10 Rules of Methodical Innovators without you having to "announce" a formal change in your style. You have given them a taste for it already, and they have responded. Thus, when you do emphasize the need for a change in their individual styles, they will be mentally prepared. The smart and aggressive ones would already have made big strides, and the rest will follow.

The sweeping change in your style and the transformation challenge call for a more formal setting of expectations, feedback, and measurement of individual alignment and performance.

Setting New Expectations and Guiding Your Team's Transformation

Before you transition into full-scale execution, it is critical to address two sides of the change coin. The first clarity: how you will lead or manage going forward? The second is expectations: how you will outline clearly what you expect from them individually and collectively? As the team gets involved in the formal scoping, prioritization, planning, and budgeting exercises, the change in style becomes clear. This cascades down into individual initiatives and the extended teams.

You have already demonstrated your new leadership style. What remains to be addressed is your expectations. It is vital that you sit down and formally outline your expectations and the need for their own transformation—individually and as a team. There are several things you can do as a leader to set a tone of seriousness, urgency, and formality in these discussions:

- Outline the concept of a data-driven approach and underline the importance of individual transformation.

- Make your team members aware of the shift from the way things were done before to a new data-driven approach.

- Illustrate from examples in Steps 1 and 2 to illustrate how viewing things through a data-only lens leads everyone to the right understanding, decisions, and outcomes.

- Encourage a culture in which saying "I don't know—how can we figure it out as a team?" engenders a collaborative and investigative culture.

- Hold regular one-on-one discussion with your direct team for individual expectation setting and feedback, given your knowledge of them.

- Provide access to knowledge sources to the entire team.

The paradox of the information age is this—the more you know as a leader, the less your teams are likely to know—unless they have access to the same knowledge sources that you do. If you subscribe to reports or rely on specific internal or external materials for guidance, share them with your team. The same knowledge sources that inform your leadership choices will be valuable to your team as well.

Having provided team member with access to knowledge, insist on a culture of coming prepared. Emphasize that ignorance about the subject is not an acceptable excuse.

- Outline your expectations from everyone as a Team.

- Set up a learning timetable for the team, with reasonable deadlines. Topics could be about analytics, new industry technologies, competitive dynamics, benchmarking, etc.

- Be formal in outlining your group-based business or operational or transformational outcomes. As far as possible, link all forms of bonus compensation and rewards to performance and adoption of principles of the new leadership style.

By setting the context for change and individual and team expectations, you place the ball in your teams' courts. By providing them with knowledge and data, you empower them.

Testing Comprehension and Acceptance of Change

It is normal business practice to measure performance at the end of a quarter or six months or a year. However, testing the learning of leaders is a novel concept. How rigorously this is implemented depends on the culture of the organization. Note that Digital Champion companies invest in role-based training and certification, i.e., they formally test their leaders and managers.

> By setting the context for change and individual and team expectations, you place the ball in your teams' courts. By providing them with knowledge and data, you empower them.

Assessments can be of two types: informal and formal. Let us look at both.

Informal Assessments (50 Percent Weight)

The interactions you have during the first three to four months will tell you how each team member is responding. The key dimensions to measure in your informal discussions are their ability and willingness to learn. Then comes their adaptability, enthusiasm, and the ability to take risks. Conversely, watch for cynicism, fear, and unwillingness to change.

Do not initiate any adverse actions prior to the end of the timeline you have set for the team. Such an action will be premature and will call into question your fairness and credibility and will also affect their belief in the program. Fear and anxiety about change are normal, but over time they are usually replaced by increasing comfort and a willingness to take risks. These are all indicators of a person who is willing to learn and grow and should be nurtured. Therefore, observe and share informal feedback as you go. Avoid taking action until after the completion of the learning timeframe and sharing formal feedback.

Formal Assessments (50 Percent Weight)

After the learning timeframe has run its course, formally assess what each member of your leadership team has internalized. Look for a foundational absorption of the techniques of a Methodical Innovator.

While counterintuitive, Methodical Leaders usually look for team members who are better than the leader in their specific roles. The logic is that when each individual is better than their leader at something, the overall team gets stronger. This leads team members to perform better and achieve goals more quickly. Methodical Innovators thus build and empower teams and do not overshadow them.

An effective way of evaluating each team member is to have them put together a presentation outlining the following six themes. While a lot of this would have been covered in the first ninety days, it is still pertinent to make each member do this formally.

- Awareness. Their understanding of digital change in the industry, company, and their individual role.

- Comprehension. What changes they feel are permanent and what may be short-term trends. What opportunities they see for innovation, acceleration, and taking the lead in an environment of change.

- Readiness. Their conclusions on current challenges, and gaps relative to where your industry and their role are headed.

- Vision and Priorities. How they see their function evolve during the next one to three years, and their priorities. It is critical to determine whether they have adopted a data-driven approach.

- Networking strategy. Assess the support they need from you, their peers, and from the company in developing their vision and executing it successfully.

- Leadership model. Identify their own new management style and decision-making processes. A self-assessment of the personal change they have experienced so far and what they still need to learn should be done.

To ensure consistency in these formal assessments, establish a rubric or evaluation metric beforehand. Use a simple numeric rating scale of 1–7.

Making the Difficult Decisions—Building the Best Team for Digital Transformation

Your informal and formal assessments will show your team members falling into four broad categories: Potential Leaders, who are adaptable and eager, Cynics, who are rigid in their thinking, Borderline Cases falling between those two, and Unable or Unwilling, those who will not adapt to change. Table 11 summarizes each of these team member types and describes the appropriate action to take.

TABLE 11. DIGITAL IQ AND LEADERSHIP EVALUATION FRAMEWORK

GROUP	DIGITAL IQ AND ATTITUDE	ACTION
Potential Leaders	Scoring 5/7 in at least four categories: These are intelligent leaders who comprehend the change, are adaptable, are energized, and have the right expertise and management techniques. These people will drive your success, lead by example, and become your ambassadors for change.	Stretch them. Give these leaders more opportunities to succeed and carefully consider their viewpoints. Their traits should be carefully assessed, and they should be supported in replicating those traits in their own teams.
Borderline Cases	Scoring 5/7 in three categories: These team members with a great attitude who lack either expertise or technique. Chances are they just need extra coaching, mentorship, access to more materials, hands-on support in the initial stages, etc.	Invest in them. Leaders with the right attitude want to succeed. Given the opportunity, they always learn and adapt. For these team members, invest in their training, development, and on-the-job coaching until they launch.
Cynics	These team members show rigidity, lack of belief, and cynicism in their performance, discussions, and team working sessions. They will not only fail in their tasks, but will negatively influence other team members, becoming a drain on you as well.	Rotate them out of your team. To successfully lead your organization across the Digital Faultline, these leaders must be phased out of your team without delay, as cynical attitudes are rarely significantly changed for people in the advanced stages of their careers. This is an unfortunate but necessary step to take.
Unable or Unwilling	These are team members who, despite your best efforts and theirs, are unable to grasp the changes ahead or the leadership style required—or who are unwilling to acknowledge and adapt as required.	Rotate them out of the organization. These leaders may have made you and the organization successful in the past, but unfortunately they are now an impediment to the future. Therefore, they must be rotated out of the organization entirely.

© Trianz 2020

Your team members' engagement as you utilize the playbook should have made a great deal of difference on each individual in the team. As a result of their experience, potential, and learning, most members of your team would be potential leaders. Those on the borderline and with the right attitude can be coached.

With the Cynics or Unwilling, personalities not known to change, you must make the necessary tough decisions or else your momentum will stall. You will fall behind deadlines and commitments—and the morale of others who are playing by the new rules and models will be adversely affected.

As a Methodical Innovator, you must be decisive in rotating out members who cannot rise to the challenge, but time your decisions correctly. You must work with HR to bring new leaders on board before you phase a team member out.

> As a Methodical Innovator, you must be decisive in rotating out members who cannot rise to the challenge, but time your decisions correctly.

During rotations and transitions, it is okay to bring in seasoned consultants on an interim basis. It is also okay to offer an opportunity to those next-level managers who are intelligent and eager to contribute. But know this: not acting or creating alternatives can be fatally damaging.

After all is said and done, the process of calibrating, aligning, and developing your direct reports into Methodical Innovators is a continuing activity and a constant process. The steps outlined in this playbook are just the beginning of the process. Much like business transformation, leadership transformation is iterative too.

Once your leaders go through an entire execution cycle, their confidence in their new style and in themselves will grow. From that point on, they will need minimal hand-holding and will grow on their own.

This is what Methodical Leaders do. They create more leaders in their mold and transform through those new leaders as opposed to doing everything themselves.

MEASURING PROGRESS AND CROSSING THE FAULTLINE

As a leader, how do you know how much progress has been made? How can you know whether the process itself is working? How can you tell if you are far enough from the Digital Faultline and have reached a zone where you are in control? These questions naturally arise for both leaders and their teams throughout the journey to cross the faultline. The only way to find out is by measuring progress.

Let us imagine for a moment that you have gone through a few iterations of execution. You have done everything that was expected of you as a leader (and more) to take your team and organization across the Digital Faultline. You have studied digitalization in your industry and its impact on your company. You have embraced a new leadership persona and fully understand your responsibilities. You developed your digital vision and priorities using data and benchmarking. You calibrated each team member's ability to transform and then rebuilt and aligned your team to match your digital vision. Finally, you have begun using the 10 Rules, and they are becoming ingrained habits. In the process, you have become a committed Methodical Innovator who targets measurable outcomes. But how do you know if you have crossed the Digital Faultline?

As your transformation progresses, the business itself changes fundamentally. Value propositions, experiences, processes, organizational structures, and financial models will continuously evolve. Therefore, what you measure must also evolve.

Let us look at an example of how this happens. Figure 37 depicts a human capital management (HCM) function that has transformed over a few strategy and execution cycles. While the labels of each major subfunction in HCM may be familiar to you, several new digital themes and capabilities emerge within each of them. These have been marked in italics. The HCM function in this example is clear about its employee value proposition. It views its employees as its customers, strives to create an employee-centric workplace, and invests in learning. It is committed to delivering a highly digitalized employee experience from start to finish.

FIGURE 37. DIGITAL HCM ORGANIZATION

Analytics & Insights	• *HCM data lakes* • *Digital KPIs* • Financial planning & budgeting	• Employee costs • Productivity analytics • Transactional analytics	• *Social analytics* • *HCM site traffic analytics* • *Big Data analytics*
Talent Acquisition & On-boarding	• *Digital sourcing* • Online skill testing • Screening	• Interview scheduling • Offer management • Background verification	• *Social media profile verification* • Employee on-boarding

Performance Management	**Learning & Development**	**Employee Engagement**
• Goal setting • Performance tracking • Performance appraisals • Promotions • High-performer acceleration	• *Virtual university* • Curriculum management • Enrollment • Training delivery • Certifications • Training Partnerships	• Organizational communications • Managerial engagement • Business events • Social events • Employee satisfaction • Corporate social responsibility

Employer Branding	**Organizational Development**	**Digital Work Places**
• *Brand social network* • Career pages • Accolades • Employee feedback • Culture framework • *HCM site experience*	• Business engagement • Organization design • Change management • Employee engagement • Communications	• *Intranet* • Knowledge management • *HCM self-service apps* • Business apps • *Enterprise digital work culture*

Digital HCM Operations	• Payroll management • Benefits management • Policy management	• HRMS • Campus operations • Record/document management

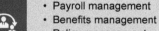

Cloud & On-Premise IT Infrastructure

Items specific to a digital HCM organization are shown above in italics

The top row of Figure 37 shows the type of analytics an HC leader must track. The breadth of analytics investment in the topmost box shows that this HC organization has evolved to become data- and insight-driven. It collects and analyzes data from the overall ecosystem (not just from within the walls of the company) using sophisticated predictive analytics capabilities. It also has a dedicated digital KPI competency, i.e., the new metrics that it uses to measure the degree of digitalization and organizational adoption.

To illustrate how the KPIs that you measure change as you digitalize your business, let us focus on a small portion of one discipline—talent acquisition. Tables 12, 13, and 14 include sample KPIs meant to convey the point; it is not an exhaustive list.

TABLE 12. CONVENTIONAL KPIs (LAGGING ONLY)

CATEGORY		KPI	METRIC
	Sourcing	Source analysis	Source of hire % (channels, costs incurred by channel)
		# of applications received from various sources	Applications/opening
		Cost of hiring	Cost/candidate
	Skill testing	Rejection ratio	Skill-based rejection %
	Interview/ hiring	Pipeline quality	Interviews/position

© Trianz 2020

TABLE 13. DIGITAL KPIs (LEADING)

CATEGORY		KPI	METRIC
	Sourcing	Evaluation of contribution/ digital source	Digitally sourced pipeline %
		Predictive source analysis	Digitally sourcing growth %
	Skill testing	Digital testing prior to interviews	% of applicants tested online
	Interview/ hiring	Pipeline management	% of candidates with automated scheduling/alerts % of interviews conducted online
		Candidate experience	% of positive feedback

© Trianz 2020

TABLE 14. DIGITAL KPIs (LAGGING)

CATEGORY		KPI	METRIC
	Sourcing	Digital sourcing effectiveness index	Hires via digital medium/total external hires
		Digital ROI analysis	Cost of digital vs. nondigital hires
		Digital referral ROI	Cost of hiring/digitally sourced candidate
	Skill testing	Digital hiring success	% of digitally hired candidates retained at six months, one year, two years Learning performance of digital vs. traditional hires
	Interview/ hiring	Hiring cycle times	Cycle time/digitally sourced candidate vs. all candidates
		Compensation	Mean/median comparison of digitally sourced vs. traditional hires
		Joining rate of digitally sourced candidates	% of digitally sourced candidates joining after selection

© Trianz 2020

As you can see, this HC organization has invested a substantial amount of effort in talent acquisition and knows what it must track. Digital KPIs begin to reveal your transition into a new way of doing things. As your team reviews the insights, it will start speaking a different language replete with leading KPIs and in competitive terms.

The best thing about creating and tracking digital KPIs in this way is that you will know whether your performance is good or bad. You will know what is working and what is not—and you will automatically target improvements to be made in future iterations.

Digital KPIs are the GPS of your status, progress, and directional alignment in your journey across the Digital Faultline.

Deploying Digital KPI Frameworks

To always know where you are, visualize where you need to be and then work backward on a plan to get there. Digital KPIs are vital. An important part of Step 2 is developing and deploying a digital KPI framework for your organization along the following lines.

Benchmark your organization's digital maturity against that of your peers. For example, a leader in sales should compare their digital maturity against the best sales organizations in the world, not just within their industry. Keep in mind that digitalization is still in its early stages; therefore, those in your industry may or may not be the best comparison. This benchmarking tells you where you stand, where your competitors are, and what the best-in-class and industry averages are worldwide.

Develop a long-term vision, but stay focused on the next iteration. As described earlier, you can either develop a long-term blueprint that you arrive at via iterations (accepting that your eventual destination may be quite different than what you envision now) or begin the first few iterations and develop a long-term plan afterward. No matter the method, clearly identify the areas that will be digitalized.

Define leading and lagging digital KPIs. For each area being digitalized, define a leading and lagging KPI or metric that is specific to your company and business. Often, these KPIs will not exist in the industry and will have to be invented. So, develop your own metrics—it can be a lot of fun!

Partner with IT to deploy an analytics platform. Work with IT to identify data sources. Automate data collection and the delivery of insights through rich real-time visualization platforms. If you have an existing platform, see whether it can be extended. If not, deploy a new one. This will be one of the best investments you will ever make as a leader.

Determine the frequency for measurement and/or review of the data. Now that you know what to measure and understand the data required to do so, review on a regular basis. Some metrics must be reviewed daily, others on a monthly or quarterly basis. The rhythm of measurements is dictated by the rhythm of the business.

Generate insights from digitalization and measure its business impact. Again, these will be specific to your role, business or function, and industry. If you are in sales, a key digital metric, "percent of sales through digital channels," will show how far you have shifted from a traditional to a digital process, from scouting, pursuing, convincing, and winning to onboarding new customers. If 20 percent of your new revenue is coming from online channels, that means you have progressed from traditional into the digital mode to that extent. Next, measure other KPIs such as conversion rate, costs, retention experience per customer acquired digitally. This absolute and relative comparison between legacy and digital models will reveal your progress. The first measures will show directional progress toward crossing the faultline.

Knowing When You Have Crossed the Digital Faultline

Back to the earlier question: "How do I know when I've crossed the Digital Faultline?" To understand whether you have crossed and sufficiently moved past the faultline and are now in a zone of control, let us remind ourselves of important concepts.

Always know your current position on the Digital Faultline. Upheavals vary by industry, company, and business or technology function—and they are continuous. Therefore, you must continuously understand the forces at work in your personal context. You will also need to know your current level of digital maturity in relation to your competitors and know what needs to happen next. Continuously tracking digital KPIs and benchmarking periodically will reveal your competitive position.

Watch for your point of digital convergence (PDC) as described extensively in Rule #9. Put simply, the PDC is a point in your evolution at which your business unit or organization reaches a Level 3 maturity. You have migrated 40–50 percent of processes, technologies, structures, and measurements into the digital paradigm. Table 15 presents these four dimensions and how they change from the faultline to the PDC.

TABLE 15. DIMENSIONS OF DIGITAL COMPETITIVENESS ON THE DIGITAL
FAULTLINE AND AT THE PDC

DIMENSIONS OF DIGITAL COMPETITIVENESS	FAULTLINE SCENARIO	PDC SCENARIO
Leadership and decision-making	Poor understanding of digital transformation and change; nervousness and a fear of the unknown	Thorough understanding of change; calm and in control; precise clarity on what to do next
	Traditional decision-making for Digital Age challenges and opportunities	Methodical Innovators, data-driven in their decision-making; measuring KPIs
Rethinking of product/service portfolios	Poor understanding of customers and internal stakeholders, their behaviors, and expectations	Knowing, tracking, and anticipating stakeholder behavior and expectations; show extreme stakeholder centricity.
	"Build it and they will come" culture	Empathy-based approach in building value propositions
Process digitalization using technology	Limited digitalization; random or sporadic initiatives	Stakeholder-driven prioritization; business outcome-centric initiatives throughout the organization
	Technology for technology's sake; poor alignment or collaboration between business and IT	Thorough understanding of technology as a vehicle for change; business and IT as equal partners
Talent and organization	Lack of skills, techniques, and experience in using digital technologies.	Serious investments in talent, before and after initiatives; technology-savvy teams, higher energy, and confidence
	Fear, doubt, and uncertainty in employee roles and over their long-term future; poor communications	Evolved organizational structures, clarity of role and performance expectations; data-supported leader communications

© Trianz 2020

As Figure 38 shows, the PDC is a critical milestone reached
after a series of iterative strategy and execution cycles. It also marks
your personal transformation into a Methodical Innovator. You will
have mastered the 10 Rules and created a group of leaders who also
transformed while executing your vision. Your team has transformed
40–50 percent of the processes. They have produced analytics that

show accomplishments and pinpoint where the gaps are. The trend lines will tell you exactly what needs to be done to attain a Level 4 maturity on the digital enterprise evolution model (DEEM). In effect, you have better control over the present.

FIGURE 38. ITERATIVE EXECUTION AND THE POINT OF DIGITAL CONVER-GENCE (PDC)

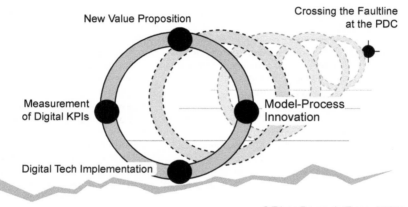

© Trianz Research (Trasers) 2021

This is when you have crossed the Digital Faultline and have reached a zone of safety and control over your organization and team's destiny. While more efforts are needed, you can look forward with no doubts about your future direction.

At the PDC, you will have a clear picture of your model and process performance. You will see new abilities in your team and their new lexicon. You will have ushered in a data-driven culture and will also know what is not working and what to do about it. All this will feel different from the traditional model—because it is.

You and your team will know what must be done to achieve the next level of maturity and will ease into the next iteration seamlessly.

THERE IS NO FINISH LINE FOR WINNERS—TRANSFORMING BEYOND THE FAULTLINE

Crossing the Digital Faultline must be celebrated as a major success, and deservedly so: it comes after grueling endeavor. A team that crosses the faultline is making strides toward become among the 7 percent of organizations—Digital Champions—that have established market leadership. At a personal level, its leaders become Methodical Innovators.

It is my fervent hope that this small group of Digital Champions will increase in size over time. I also hope that most of these companies will turn the tide on the hi-tech industry's relentless onslaught on their turfs. One endeavor of this book is the furthering of that reversal. But even as you cross the Digital Faultline, it is important to remember that there is no such thing as an end state. This is not a project with an end date.

As we have seen throughout this book, industries and companies will continuously evolve with changing B2C or B2B customer behavior. Disruptive technologies will bring in new value propositions and new regulations. Add to that the constantly changing employee behaviors and expectations. Then add COVID-19 and its impact on economic and business models. Every one of these factors will change continuously and accelerate digitalization.

Two clear patterns will emerge when a team crosses the Digital Faultline. The first is the difference between pushing to change vs. being pulled by change, with the second, the concept of digital shifts. These are complex topics for another day, but I will briefly touch upon them here. The idea is to show why there are no completed or final digital transformations—only digital transitions.

Pushing for Change vs. Being Pulled by Change

Until you reach the PDC and cross the Digital Faultline, you and your team are pushing forward. First pushing yourselves, then your peers in the company, and finally, your extended team and your IT partners. You are constantly advocating a new customer and stakeholder centricity and a data-driven decision-making culture. You are pushing new points of view and convincing everyone about what the change is, why it is needed, and why you must make the transition now. You are, therefore, a crusader in the truest sense of the word—one who is constantly pushing for change.

A breathtaking reversal takes place once a team crosses the Digital Faultline. The results do the talking, and leaders no longer have to convince anyone of anything. They exhale, having been released from the push efforts, and their team now fully gets the transformation game. They will operate with a higher level of confidence and at a much increased velocity.

Why does this reversal from pushing to pulling take place? Given your new digital KPI frameworks, you will automatically know what the set of next priorities and issues are. You know how your teams perform and how to organize leadership for the next cycle. As you review your successful performance against the competition through benchmarking, the pace accelerates. Your team will now be propelled—pulled by change. At this point, your business is in a constant state of proactive evolution, pulled by internal forces such performance indicators and organizational ambition. Your team are also pulled by external forces such as customers, market opportunities, technologies, and competition.

Methodical Innovators keep their teams focused on forward movement by responding to the pull effect of these forces. Contrarily, the more traditional a company and the larger the legacy business, the more they recoil to old ways. This backlash could take the shape of politics, lobbying, internal competition, or resistance to change. Leaders and teams that resist this pull, succumb to internal backlash, or are unable to keep up with their competitors will fall by the wayside.

Smart leaders anticipate this pushback and do everything they can to proactively respond and prevent it. Again, data-driven insights are their best friends. Those who show relentlessness will deliver results that will be acknowledged by peers and superiors alike.

The pull of change after crossing the Digital Faultline will evolve toward market leadership.

New Physics of Digital Transformations

TGTS data revealed some interesting insights about how industries will evolve. As discussed in Part I—The Stages of Digital

> Smart leaders anticipate this pushback and do everything they can to proactively respond and prevent it. Again, data-driven insights are their best friends. Those who show relentlessness will deliver results that will be acknowledged by peers and superiors alike.

Evolution, companies in all industries will evolve across five major levels. However, given that the forces act differently, each industry's starting point, pace, and direction will also be different. But governed by the underlying rules, everything will evolve.

This physics of digitalization is illustrated in Figure 39, where time is added to the x-axis and the scope of digitalization to the y-axis. For example, when the average level of digitalization in an industry goes from Level 2 to Level 4 in six years, we can say that the industry's digital velocity is one level per every three years. Since digital evolution is continuous, today's Level 5 will eventually be tomorrow's Level 1.

**FIGURE 39. TRIANZ DIGITAL ENTERPRISE EVOLUTION MODEL (DEEM)©
WITH TIME AND SCOPE**

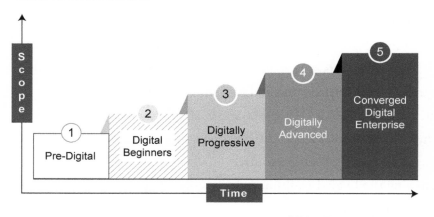

© Trianz Research (Trasers) 2021

Let me illustrate this with the example of the auto industry.

In a span of three decades, we have gone from diesel- and gasoline-powered cars to hybrid cars and then to electric cars. Tesla has evolved to electric and driverless cars. Auto companies producing electric self-driving cars are the Level 5 Converged Digital Enterprises of today.

The next level of evolution will be electric and driverless cars and eventually pilotless flying cars. These will be controlled by computers and ground operations. Though this sounds far-fetched, just look at Lillum, in Germany—a company that has successfully produced and flight-tested an all-electric personal vertical takeoff vehicle. Its wings fold inward, and it can be stored in a typical homeowner's backyard. Toyota is not too far behind. When this happens, the auto industry will have evolved. They are no longer machines that only drive on four wheels on the earth's surface but something completely different.

We will also begin to see industry collisions. Who will win the battle between the auto giants (GM, BMW, Mercedes, Fiat, Tesla, Toyota, Hyundai, and Tata) and the aerospace companies (Airbus, Boeing, Embraer, Lockheed-Martin, Grumman, Saab, and Cessna)? How will Apple, Microsoft, Google, Netflix, and Disney elbow their way in? Or will completely new start-ups, like Lillium, create a flying Tesla? What impact will flying cars have on where people live and work, how commercial and residential real estate is bought and sold? How will global transportation infrastructure be configured?

The questions can be overwhelming. In this example, an electric car may be Level 5 today but may be obsolete when flying cars become the norm. In other words, the Level 5 of today will be a Level 1 of tomorrow. That is when the auto industry—its consumers, products, services, experiences, and ecosystems—will have gone through more than a 100 percent change. That is what I call as digital shift of an industry.

No Finish Line for Digital Winners

No matter where we are born, we are raised in conventional paradigms of starting, progressing, and finishing. For every event, we are accustomed to seeing a finish—the end of a one-hundred-meter sprint, a marathon, a dance recital, a project or a technology implementation, and so on. The race is always over when you cross the finish line.

But digital transformation is about continuous change, and what is Level 5 maturity today will be obsolete tomorrow. In this new normal, there will not be any finish lines for winners. Companies that cannot visualize a new future and do not let go of outdated products, services, and business models will be ignored by customers. Those that are unwilling to adapt to new cultures and ways of doing things will perish. From the Walkman to the VCR, we have seen numerous long-standing companies and iconic brands fade into oblivion when they stopped innovating. Their dominant market presence and immense financial strength simply did not matter.

Given that change is continuous, you as a leader must abandon any thought of crossing a finish line. Stop asking yourself "When will this end?"—because it will not. Crossing the Digital Faultline is simply a milestone on the path to getting ahead of change and beating future shock.

Leaders as Stewards of Cultures: Defining Personal Success beyond the Crossing

For a company that has not yet transitioned, it is impossible to predict or visualize what any industry might look like ten to fifteen years. The first focus of today's leaders must be getting their organizations across the Digital Faultline. The clearer you are about this vision, the harder you will drive execution while building well-aligned leadership teams.

Companies in a position of industry leadership will foresee changes and may even define what those changes are. When you get to the competitive position held by Amazon, Microsoft, Apple, Netflix, Disney, and Tesla, you will keep leading in your industry. While the rest of your industry plays catch-up, you will be busy defining the future (Figure 40).

FIGURE 40. LEADERS AS STEWARDS

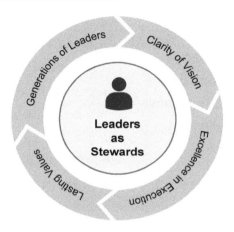

© Trianz Research (Trasers) 2021

It is a long, arduous journey to get to that industry leadership position. These companies took more than twenty-five years to achieve their status. A principal reason for their success is not their transformation to a new end state. Rather, their top leadership understood that, given that transformations are continuous, their role is to act as stewards of competitive cultures. They had great clarity of vision as to what they wanted their company or organization to be. They built teams that excelled in execution and developed systems of lasting value. And finally, they created organizational models and cultures that produced generations of leaders.

My sincere advice to every senior leader reading this book is to stay extremely focused on crossing the Digital Faultline—and keep in mind what not to do. For instance, do not overthink the concept of the Digital Age because it will only get more complex as it unfolds. Do not craft a ten-to-fifteen-year vision or plan; the variables will change every few years. And do not attempt to do too many things at once—you will exhaust yourself.

> Do not craft a ten-to-fifteen-year vision or plan; the variables will change every few years. And do not attempt to do too many things at once—you will exhaust yourself.

The most urgent and valuable contribution of your career will be to help your organization to cross the Digital Faultline first. Then become a steward of vision, execution models, and values, and set your organization on course for digital leadership. In the process, you will create and empower a new generation of leaders from within. For any leader, transitioning their company into the Digital Age and passing the baton to that next generation will be two achievements to be proud of.

APPENDIX

Trianz Global Transformation Survey (TGTS) Methodology

When my company began studying digital transformations, I said that data should be the cornerstone of all things Trianz. In that, we committed to developing insights on statistically significant data on digital transformations gathered globally from multiple industries and companies of various sizes. We launched the Trianz Global Transformation Survey (TGTS), a series of tailored surveys in multiple languages covering every major business and IT function worldwide.

In the process, Trianz has created a massive global digital-transformation database with more than 1.5 million data points across twenty industries, which powers all our research.

Role-Specific Surveys

TGTS role-specific surveys had five hundred to nine hundred respondents each, for a total of over nine thousand respondents from over five thousand unique companies around the world. Respondents across the leadership of an enterprise were screened based on their functional role, title, industry, region, and company size.

TGTS was comprised of the following sixteen role-specific surveys of decision-makers with titles of director or above:

- CEO

- R&D and Innovation

- Sales

- Marketing

- Service Management (customer experience/customer service)

- Supply Chain Management

- Human Capital Management (human resources)

- Manufacturing/Production

- Finance and Accounting

- Procurement

- Legal

- Chief Information Officer (CIO)

- Analytics IT

- Digital/Business Applications IT

- Cloud IT

- Security IT Functions

- Survey Themes

We collected respondents' perspectives on digital transformations ranging across vision, strategy, priorities, implementation, technologies, and change management. Sample survey topics included:

- Definition and role of digital transformation by functional role
- Strategy and process for digital-transformation initiatives
- Digital-transformation maturity by role and subfunctions
- Technology investments and future priorities in digital transformation by function
- Technology usage, engineering models, and support
- Impact of COVID-19 on business, customers, organization, business continuity, and digital transformations
- Workforce readiness and training
- Leadership and culture of change

Industry Coverage

Respondents spanned eighteen industries in the original survey waves, and new industries are added each year:

- Automotive
- Banking
- Construction and infrastructure
- Consumer products
- Energy
- Financial services
- Food and beverages
- Health insurance
- Healthcare
- Hi-tech

- Industrial manufacturing

- Life insurance

- Logistics

- Media and entertainment

- Property and casualty insurance

- Pharmaceuticals

- Reinsurance

- Retail

- Telecommunications

- Travel and hospitality

This industry-specific data can be seen in Figure 4: Change state of digital transformation across industries and in Figure 13: 2019 industry positioning quadrant—cloud adoption by hi-tech.

Geography and Size

TGTS is a truly global survey, with respondents spanning six regions of the world: North America, South America, UK and EU, Middle East and Africa, Asia-Pacific, and Australia-New Zealand. A sample of region-specific survey data can be seen in Figure 2: Time to market for new product launch.

TGTS includes respondents from companies of all sizes: small businesses (fifty to five hundred employees), medium businesses (five hundred to one thousand employees), emerging enterprises (one thousand to five thousand employees), and large enterprises (over five thousand employees).

Survey Administration

TGTS has been administered in several waves, starting in 2018 and continuing today, in the respondents' original language. Multiple methodologies for data collection are employed, depending on the market, including phone interviews (CATI, computer-assisted telephone interviewing), online surveys (CAWI, computer-assisted web interviewing), and a hybrid of in-person and online surveys.

The resulting data file was scrubbed of incomplete responses and "straight liners" (where the respondent chooses, for example, answer A for every question) to ensure data quality).

Trianz follows the most stringent privacy standards; data is analyzed only in aggregate, and no individual- or company-level data is revealed to our researchers or our clients.

TGTS is ISO 9000 Certified

TGTS is ISO 9001 certified and demonstrates Trianz's commitment to an effective quality management system via continual, rigorous research processes and services. All our processes—from primary data collection, quality assurance, and privacy and security of information to analysis and insight generation—comply with ISO 9001 standards.

TUV (Technischer Überwachungsverein) audited and certified Trianz in 2018 via an intensive evaluation process that included quality management system development, a management system documentation review, preaudit, initial assessment, and clearance. The certification validates the consistency and accuracy in our end-to-end process.

ABOUT THE AUTHOR

Sri Manchala is the Chairman and CEO of Trianz, a digital transformation services firm serving leading global corporations across multiple industries. *Crossing the Digital Faultline* is a combination of Sri's 23 years of experience in technology based in Silicon Valley, extensive research, and ongoing partnerships with senior clients during their transformations.

Sri's professional path toward technology has been anything but conventional. A graduate of the National Defense Academy, one of the world's elite training institutions for Armed Forces officers, Sri served in the Indian Army in the Infantry and Parachute Regiment–Special Forces. Transitioning into the corporate world, Sri joined Asian Paints, India's largest paint and chemicals manufacturer, for a brief period. In 1995, Sri studied international business, corporate strategy, and organizational development at the IBEAR MBA Program at the University of Southern California's Marshall School of Business in Los Angeles, where he is now a Corporate Advisory Board Member.

Sri joined the high-tech strategy and supply chain consulting practice of KPMG in the firm's Silicon Valley office. He later joined Cisco Systems at the company's headquarters, which allowed him to further practice and learn the processes of strategic and fast-paced operational evolution of a pioneering giant in the technology industry.

In 2001, he founded Silicon Valley-based Trianz, launching an operations transformation practice as the first internet wave was emerging. Abstracting several concepts from his military experience, Sri shaped a unique model, culture, and team commitment at Trianz which even today helps clients evolve strategically while achieving the best business outcomes from their technology investments.

Beginning in 2016, Sri, along with the Trianz leadership team, guided the company's transition into a highly focused digital transformation strategy, execution, and managed services company. Trianz continues to serve leading corporations, winning industry recognition and numerous awards, including being named to *Forbes* magazine's "America's Best Management Consulting Firms" list for three consecutive years.

Crossing the Digital Faultline is a synthesis of insights from the Trianz Global Transformation Surveys which collected over 1.5 million datapoints from 5,000-plus companies; Sri and Trianz's experience over hundreds of technology engagements and numerous discussions with clients. In this synthesis, Sri concludes that the two most critical elements in a team or an organization's successful transformation is their digital IQ (about the new rules of the game) and the character of its individual and collective leadership. In outlining a new concept and approach for Digital Age leadership, Sri also applies principles he learned in the military.

Crossing the Digital Faultline is Sri Manchala's contribution to every business and technology leader aspiring to get away from the chaos companies are experiencing due to the duality of digitalization and COVID-19 uncertainties, to a point of stability, control, and command over the future of their organizations.

ACKNOWLEDGMENTS

Writing this book was more difficult and yet more rewarding than I could have imagined. It is my sincere hope that sharing data analyses, experiences, and lessons learned will help others through challenging and confusing times with clarity and purpose. None of this would have been possible without the incredible support and encouragement from my wife Laxmi and our family, who allowed me to stay focused on this goal despite challenging circumstances, and for forgiving the times spent away from them all.

Dr. Arvind Bhambri, distinguished professor of strategy at the Marshall School of Business at the University of Southern California, whose unmatched expertise and dedication to finding truth through data guided the exceptional digital transformation research.

A very special thank you to the entire research and analytics staff at Trianz for the intense research and incredible quality of large volume data they provided to support the correlations and insights described in this book.

The valuable experience-based insights graciously provided by our exceptional Trianz clients continue to drive us toward excellence, and I am indebted to them all for their transparency and honest feedback.

Needing a specialized environment to gather data and insights, I am grateful to the University of Southern California International Business Education and Research MBA program at the Marshall School of Business, for allowing the use of their facilities for research.

To the 9,000+ business and IT leaders from around the world who gave their time to contribute data supporting this research, and for being open to sharing information that helps others succeed, I thank you.

I am deeply thankful to Prashant Bhavaraju, Vice President at Trianz, for his valuable input, tireless commitment, daily sacrifices, and the incredible orchestration that led to this book's production.

Many thanks to the Forbes|Advantage Books team—Alison Morse, Kristin Goodale, Tracy Hill and Courtney Morrill for their dedication to high quality and smooth execution of the process. My deep gratitude to editors Stephen Larkin and Ann Hanson for simplifying and elevating it.

Finally, to all readers, thank you for entrusting me to guide you on the journey across the Digital Faultline. May your successes be many!

Lightning Source UK Ltd.
Milton Keynes UK
UKHW012011270721
387847UK00002B/692